6/24/16

Bev and D

Great to be with you two on Chunk adven. Hope you can make it to Vermont.

It's all about Faith + Trust.

Richard Cashion

The Road From Troas

A Legacy Letter Of Faith & Trust

W. Richard Cashion Jr., M.D.

Copyright © 2016 W. Richard Cashion Jr., M.D.

All rights reserved. No part of this book may be used or reproduced by any means, graphic, electronic, or mechanical, including photocopying, recording, taping or by any information storage retrieval system without the written permission of the author except in the case of brief quotations embodied in critical articles and reviews.

Scripture quotations taken from the New American Standard Bible®, Copyright © 1960, 1962, 1963, 1968, 1971, 1972, 1973, 1975, 1977, 1995 by The Lockman Foundation. Used by permission. (www.Lockman.org)

WestBow Press books may be ordered through booksellers or by contacting:

WestBow Press
A Division of Thomas Nelson & Zondervan
1663 Liberty Drive
Bloomington, IN 47403
www.westbowpress.com
1 (866) 928-1240

Because of the dynamic nature of the Internet, any web addresses or links contained in this book may have changed since publication and may no longer be valid. The views expressed in this work are solely those of the author and do not necessarily reflect the views of the publisher, and the publisher hereby disclaims any responsibility for them.

Any people depicted in stock imagery provided by Thinkstock are models, and such images are being used for illustrative purposes only. Certain stock imagery © Thinkstock.

ISBN: 978-1-5127-3148-4 (sc)
ISBN: 978-1-5127-3149-1 (hc)
ISBN: 978-1-5127-3147-7 (e)

Library of Congress Control Number: 2016902486

Print information available on the last page.

WestBow Press rev. date: 04/08/2016

Contents

Preface vii
Chapter 1 – Background 1
Chapter 2 – The Beginning and Family History 6
Chapter 3 – Early School 10
Chapter 4 – College Years 13
Chapter 5 – The Medical School Years 18
Chapter 6 – Internship Residency Training 25
Chapter 7 – Cardiology Fellowship 44
Chapter 8 – Chief Resident Year: Back to Boston 50
Chapter 9 – The Air Force Years 56
Chapter 10 – The Waco Years 60
Chapter 11 – The Houston Years 64
Chapter 12 – The College Station Years 82
Chapter 13 – The Salado Years 115
Chapter 14 – The Troas Concept 130
Chapter 15 – The New Job: Three in One 135
Conclusion 147
About the Author 149

Preface

Our system of health care has changed dramatically over the past seventy years. I feel it has not been for the good of the patients we serve or for the health care providers that toil in our current environment. My life has given me opportunities to deliver health care in every type of situation. I feel this makes me uniquely qualified to provide commentary and hopefully develop a concept to help redirect the downhill course of the profession I love.

My unique exposure to all types of medical practice has resulted in the writing of this book. I feel there is a common thread of hope to be found among medical professionals; it is love for the people we care for and passion for dealing with interesting biological situations that can be altered for the betterment of those people.

My story is really a love story about my relationship with God and four amazing women: my mother, sister, Pam, and Cindy. It is also a love story of the profession that I have been a part of for forty-nine years. It's a story about a boy with learning disabilities who survived the brutal world of medical education because of that love. It's a story of my awakening to that fact and where that love has led me.

So what's the problem with medical care today? Why is health care falling apart in the USA? I believe it is because of a lack of love for God and a lack of realization that we can't make it through this crazy system on our own. These factors have led to the decline of health care. If our health care system is more concerned about finances than love of patients, it will not be successful. This story shows how the health insurance concept and the hope for financial gains have contributed to the down-fall.

There are treads of hope that the love that made the practice of medicine great in the past can be redeveloped. We must develop a stronger bond among those who love our profession to foster a united concept to stop our downhill course. This book will lead you through a life spent strengthening those bonds and will show how that led to great success in my life. It's about developing a concept that I believe to be a gift from God: the Troas concept.

I was initially educated in the conservative southwest and completed my education in the liberal northeast. I have practiced medicine in the armed forces during a time of war, been in a small group practice as well as a large academically affiliated practice, and started a solo practice and grew it into a complete cardiovascular program with heart surgery and coronary interventions. I have been closely involved with administration of several hospitals. In 2005, I started one of the early programs doing coronary interventions without surgical back at a community hospital. I have been involved with building a hospital from an idea to a completed facility that has a four-star CMS rating. I retired but was later called back to the Veteran's

Hospital to help the wounded warriors whom I feel so close to. All these things were gifts from God. I feel I must lead you through my life to establish credibility for the concept I will present. As stated, I feel this concept was a gift from God and has led me to share things with you that many people don't know or understand about me.

This book, however, is not so much about me as it is about the grace that God demonstrated in my life. In this book, I use the term "miracle" frequently. Some will say, "Oh, those were only blessings." I agree they were blessings but of such an incredible nature, I wonder if they were not miracles. I say the difference between a blessing and a miracle is only the magnitude of the demonstration. My life has been filled with so many unexpected and near impossible happenings that I must call them miracles. Many of the events I will describe were out of the realm of possibilities and, therefore, are miracles in my mind. Read the book and decide for yourself.

This book initially started as a legacy letter to my grandchildren. As time passed and my life changed direction, I felt God was guiding me to do something bigger. The writing of his work began in approximately 2008. After seven years and several failed attempts, the book is finally making its way into the hands of readers. My hope is they find the Troas concept helpful in their own lives.

CHAPTER 1

Background

Have you ever been asked, "If you had it to do over again, would you change anything in your life?" In recalling my life, I can list several episodes that created a lot of unrest and concern; however, in retrospect, I realize they all occurred to guide me to where God wanted me to be today.

While on vacation in July 2008, I heard a sermon regarding being trapped by God. As an example, the priest used the book of Exodus to illustrate his point. God had led the Israelites into a trap where Pharaoh was behind them and the Red Sea was in front of them. Approximately three million Jews were in danger of slaughter or having to return to slavery. They were rescued to demonstrate God's power and glory.

God occasionally leads us into a trap to make us rely on His power and glory. Our medical care system has been led into a trap that many feel has no escape. Our escape will be a process requiring faith and trust. I have learned that when things are at their worst, God is the closest. You just need to look and listen for Him. He is waiting for us to trust Him and to accept the challenge to demonstrate His glory. I hope my life experiences will help people during difficult times feel closer to God and look to Him for deliverance. I feel the Troas concept is a mechanism of deliverance for our current health care system.

I was writing this book for my grandchildren to tell them the story of my life; it has turned into something much bigger. I believe God is leading me to develop a revolutionary concept to change the way health care is delivered. I know all of my grandchildren have great faith, and I hope this book will increase their faith. At least this book will make them aware of my faith journey. I am also hopeful it will start a revolution in health care delivery. It may even convince non-believing readers that there is a God and that He loves us and performs many amazing events in our lives. Most times, we have to be alert to see or feel the influence of God in these events. My life is a series of incredible happenings that have taught me to recognize the gifts from God. My first experience occurred when I was in my early fifties. I hope this book will help others realize that God does speak to all of us and works miracles in all our lives; they just often go unrecognized or are attributed to luck.

I was around fifty-four years of age before I learned to listen and realize that God was working in my life. It seems reasonable to start this story with my awakening to the Lord. My Protestant brethren would refer to this as a conversion. I have always been a spiritual and faith-filled person, but I never truly appreciated God speaking to me until I began to notice many sequences of events that happened seemingly at random and in some cases under great duress. In retrospect, these all turned out to be good.

This book was written to relate those events to my life's direction and demonstrate the influence of God and how those events led me to the Troas concept. I hope to allow people to appreciate how God may also speak to them. Writing this book has led me to develop a concept of health care delivery that I will describe in the last part of this book. But first you need to learn the things in my life that led to this concept of health care and why I feel so strongly about it. In my mind, it is based on incredible events that I feel were miracles.

People should record their life experiences for their family. I feel it is important for children to know and understand their family history and realize what directed the lives of their ancestors. I hope some members of my family will take up this torch when I am gone and record events in their lives to show how God has spoken to them. It has taken a long time for me to be brave enough to share some of the incredible things that have happened. I share them with you for the glory of God. In reading about these things, I hope you will come to appreciate how I believe all my accomplishments were gifts from God. None of them would have happened if He had not made them happen!

The consideration of recording a family history was most clearly brought to my attention during a spring break around 1985. My family at that time consisted of Pam, Trey, Jarrod, Hade, Christopher, and multiple friends. It has grown since then. We were all at our condominium at Walden on Lake Conroe. We had brought all the boys and their friends to have a good spring break of eating and water skiing. I also wanted to bring my father. He liked to be called Doc. We brought him along so he wouldn't be by himself in Houston, so we rented an efficiency apartment for him to escape the noise.

One night I got a call. "Dick, I'm having a heart attack." I went to be with him. Doc was a physician who had advanced aggressive cancer of the prostate. He knew what was going on and that his prognosis was not good. I started to call an ambulance, but he said, "No!" He told me he could tolerate the pain, and he just wanted to talk.

We talked all night. I learned things about him and my mother that I had not known. It was one of the best nights I ever had with my father. Doc continued to refuse to have medical aid, and we returned to our home in Houston the following day.

Pam and I had made plans to go to San Francisco for the American College of Physicians Meeting. I told Dad we had decided to remain in Houston, but he would not hear of it. He said, "You will not cancel the trip," so Pam and I went to the meeting. Doc died peacefully in his sleep while we were gone.

I will never forget the night we had our all-night conversation. This brought up the question "How can I tell my life story to all six of my children and my four daughters-in-law, whom I consider my daughters, which equals ten children, not to mention the fifteen grandchildren?" It became obvious that I needed to write a book so all of the children who wanted to know would have access to the story. I have been so blessed in so many ways that it seems only fitting to write a book that tells the history of my life and how God's glory made it possible for me to accomplish the many wonderful things that He has allowed me to do.

I had been reading the book written by Saint Teresa of Ávila. She cautions that one might need some spiritual advice when trying to interpret or explain events in one's life. I therefore spent a night with a Catholic priest for advice before proceeding any further with my intent to share my story. After I told him my story, he commented that I had felt the finger of God in my life.

In approximately 1995, I was giving a lecture at Texas A&M University to the Christian Medical and Dental Society. The society knew of my Christian beliefs and my feeling that spirituality should be a part of medical practice. Its representatives had asked me to share with them how I had accomplished my goals in life. I was telling my life story when I suddenly realized my whole life had been like the pieces of a puzzle. It suddenly all come together. I understood the power and love for my Lord Jesus Christ. I realized the Holy Spirit had directed all of these events. I felt God was speaking to me.

I will begin my story, and I hope and pray it will glorify God. That is my intent. What I tell you is to witness to His using my life for His glory. I truly believe that all of the events I will describe are gifts from God and not of my doing.

CHAPTER 2

The Beginning and Family History

I was born in Brooklyn, New York, on October 7, 1941. My father was physician, and my mother was a nurse. I was baptized as an infant at a Catholic church and had a very loving, faith-filled mother. At the time, my father was Protestant, but he attended church with us each Sunday. Later he became Catholic. My mother had a profound influence on my spiritual life. She was a cradle Catholic. She said prayers with me every night until I was in high school. Yes, we were on our knees before going to sleep! I therefore learned the power of prayer.

My mother was famous for helping people find things. She would pray intercessory prayers to Saint Anthony to ask Jesus to find a lost item. The lost things could be anything, such as finding a way to pass an examination, finding car keys, or whatever. It was amazing how often the correct answer arrived.

As a child, I had great difficulty in school. There were countless prayers to help me find my way through the difficult school times. In fact, I was such a poor reader that I hated being called upon to read aloud in school. My father spent countless hours helping me with my homework. He was a very kind person and taught me how to work with people from all walks of life.

All my life, I wanted to be a physician. I was told and knew I had to work harder to accomplish this goal. One of the many gifts I was given by God was a desire to succeed at being a physician. Because of this drive, I was able to discipline myself to put my studies first. After school, I would come home and begin studying. Homework was always completed before I allowed myself time to do anything "fun."

When I was in approximately the seventh grade, my mother made a deal with me not to play football and to instead make golf my sport. The deal was that she would take me to the golf course every day after school and then I would come home for my studies. She was afraid I might injure my hands and not be able to be a surgeon! The physically strenuous afternoon workouts would also make studying at night difficult.

I remember my mother helping me with my temper. She would frequently wait in the parking lot and observe me playing golf. I remember the distant car honking when I would display my anger by throwing a golf club. I learned to scout the horizon for my mother's car before demonstrating any anger. This gradually improved my reaction to adverse events. This is another gift that helped me all my life. I have learned that nothing done in anger results in anything good.

My mother always encourage me to be the best that I could be; however, she never pushed things that she felt I could not achieve. She commonly stated the goal of my life should be to always strive to be the best at whatever I could be. She would frequently say, "If you're going to be a ditch digger, be the best ditch digger you can be."

I also had a very loving sister, Mary Jane. She was two years older and was always encouraging in all my efforts. When I arrived in high school, her friends were amazed that Mary Jane's brother was actually two years younger. She'd always referred to me in such a way that they thought I must be an older brother.

At one point Mary Jane wanted to be a professional dancer and, of course, younger brother was happy to help with the dance lessons. My mother again was insistent that dancing, like golf, would serve me well all of my life. My sister and I became good dancers and entered competitive dancing when I was thirteen and she was fifteen. Two or three years later, we entered a major competition for the Arthur Murray School of Dance, the Southwest Dance Championship. We lived in Lubbock, Texas, at the time and went to Dallas to the Adolphus Hotel to enter the dancing championship. Dancers came from everywhere. It was much like the TV show *Dancing with the Stars*. All the students danced with their instructors. When they were announcing the winners for first, second, and third place, they declared Mary Jane had won second place. As she stood up to walk to the stage and receive her trophy, she bent over and whispered in my ear, "You are the best, regardless of who wins first." A few minutes later, the first place was announced: "Dick Cashion is the winner!"

You can imagine returning to Lubbock—a very Texan town—as a boy named "Dick" and a dancing champion. Both of these labels seemed to be plagues at the time, but both made me stronger, which helped me overcome life's trials.

CHAPTER 3

Early School

My serious reading problem and being the fifth man on a four-man golf team cause me multiple struggles at school. All of these things lead to a strong feeling of inferiority. My sister and mother, however, refused to buy into this and instead encourage me to run for student council.

Each class had a president and several vice presidents. I managed to become one of the sophomore vice presidents, mainly because my sister was "queen of everything" and a senior cheerleader. My position subsequently carried me on to win a junior-year vice president slot. Going into my senior year, I decided to run for president of the class. After a hard-fought campaign, I lost to a very popular person. My mother and sister stepped up again, saying, "Don't worry. Your friends will always remember you tried." The winner of the election was subsequently disqualified for "playing hooky" (an unexcused school absence to go fishing with friends). I therefore became president of the senior class by default! This taught me to "keep your slate clean" and not get discouraged over seemingly discouraging events.

Later in my senior year, it came time to apply for college. All the college-educated Cashion men had gone to Rice University in Houston. Rice University required excellent academics for admission; I clearly did not make it.

I took my entrance exam for the University of Texas. In those days, it was a test given specifically by the University of Texas. The results were disastrous! They were so bad that my father asked one of his physician friends to break the news about my future. I remember this physician telling me, "You did so poorly on the entrance exam to the University of Texas, you should change your mind about becoming a physician!" I remember telling him thanks for the advice but with the help of God I would succeed. My mother was dying from cancer of the breast, but with every bit of her fading energy she convinced me to "not give up because of a crazy exam!" I was accepted to the University of Texas. This was one of the many blessings or miracles in my life.

I went to the summer orientation program in Austin in the summer of 1959. That changed my life forever! Again, I no longer believe in coincidences or luck; I feel these incidents are God working! While standing in a cafeteria line at Kinsolving dorm, a beautiful, very talkative young lady came up to me and introduced herself as Pam King. My name tag stated that I was from Lubbock, Texas. She told me she had a good friend named Susan Ford who lived in Lubbock. Susan Ford was a good friend of mine from student council and lived one block from my home. What a "coincidence" that I had been part of student council.

My relationship with Pam started as a great friendship. It quickly turned into love. Several years later, Pam would become my wife! There are no coincidences, just God working in my life.

I returned home from orientation excited about this girl and eager to tell my mother. However, I found my mother critically ill. My mother died before I could share with her my happiness. I did not tell her about Pam, because I had already been unlucky with girlfriends in the past and felt she would only worry about me and another failure.

My mother died August 22,1959, only a few weeks before I started college. I had to prepare for going away to school. My sister stepped in to help me get ready for college. Mary Jane helped me buy all the necessary items I needed and helped me pack them. She even sewed name labels in all my clothing. She made many arrangements that I would have never been able to accomplish in my grief-stricken state.

Mary Jane had had a dream shortly after my mother's death. She shared it with me. In the dream, Mary Jane saw that mother was very happy and was told that our mother was in a better place and not to worry. I interpreted the dream to mean that our mother was in heaven and that I would now have my personal "saint" praying to Jesus for me.

CHAPTER 4

College Years

The loss of my mother was devastating! God, however, quickly filled the hole caused by my loss with my new girlfriend, Pam King. Pam was even more faith filled than I, and she helped me to grow in spirit. At the time, she was considering entering the Dominican religious life. It looks like I changed those plans. She was extremely bright and an excellent student. Her ability to study briefly and still make excellent grades never ceased to amaze me. It pushed me even harder to complete my studies early so I could join her and her family for their typical late-night dinners (which were typically held around nine or ten at night).

Pam was also a premed student, so we had some classes together; however, she was in Plan II Honors and therefore had many classes that I was unable to enroll in. She always did better than me in school, making As effortlessly.

We began to talk about marriage during our sophomore year in college. It would be a two-physician family. Pam's father ("Big Thunder"), however, brought us back to earth and suggested we wait until my second or third year in medical school before getting married. Pam was always big on "offering hardships up for God to use for greater good" (the Little Flower approach of Saint Thérèse of Lisieux). We offered up that five-year wait for a wonderful marriage, and God answered our prayers.

Our sophomore year at the University of Texas was very difficult. We probably studied harder than ever in our lives and still did not do so well, making mostly Bs and a few As. Pam and I were very involved with St. Austin's Catholic Church. We became members of the Legion of Mary. A Paulist priest became a close friend and helped us in our spiritual development. There were two problems that year that should have prevented me from getting into medical school. Both occurred the second semester.

I started out at the University of Texas as a math major. Math had always been easy for me. In fact, I arrived at UT with six hours of credits I had earned by passing the exams in algebra and geometry. I had problems with differential equations, but the real problem occurred with Theory of Equations. I was totally lost in this course. My final grade was F. The other disaster in that sophomore year was the second semester of sophomore English. We used to leave postcards with the professor at the final exam so they could send us our final grade. There was no Internet or other means of getting one's grade before it was posted on the transcript, which could take a while. When I received the postcard for sophomore English, it was quite alarming. "You made an A in this course. However, your spelling is so bad, I am giving you an F. If you take the remedial spelling course given by the English Department and make an A, I will give you your A." I took the course and my grade was an A.

With many prayers, we survived the sophomore year. Because of the grace of God, I never lost hope of becoming a physician. I kept remembering my mother's words, "Always work to be the best you can at whatever you become." My hope of becoming a physician never died, but I wondered if I would be the best.

We then started one of our hardest years, the junior year. I was taking Quantitative Analysis, a chemistry course required as a premedical requisite. It was a very difficult course, and I'm sure it was designed to weed out unqualified premedical students. Despite intense studying, I scored a 55 percent on the first exam. When I received my exam back, I began again to have serious doubts that I would make it to medical school. Pam's confidence in me and our priest friend's many prayers resulted in my final grade of B. My hope continued.

Pam developed chorioretinitis that year and almost became blind. Faced with this ailment and a heavy load of classes, she decided she had no other choice than to drop out of school. It changed her mind about being a physician. She never missed a beat, though, and stated I should try to go to medical school after only three years at Texas, despite my less-than-perfect grades, so we could get married sooner. She never doubted that I would get accepted to medical school and become a physician. This was a great idea, except it was already October of 1961 and applications for the 1962 medical school classes would close in January 1962. We hurried to get everything accomplished while Pam was recovering her vision. The University of Texas Medical Branch at Galveston and Southwestern Medical School in Dallas had programs that would accept students after three years of college; they were my only options for class in 1962.

At the time, I was selling shoes at Dacy's Shoe Store on the "Drag" at UT to make extra money. It was a great job, and I did quite well. I needed some letters of recommendation for my medical school application. Pam was with me when I asked the manager of the shoe store if he could write the letter. He said that he didn't know how to write such a letter and asked Pam if she could write the letter. He said he would read it, and if he agreed with what she said, he would sign it and I could use that as a letter of recommendation. He told her to include the fact that I was the hardest working college student he had ever employed. He stated that if hard work was required to become a physician, then I would certainly do well.

We mailed the applications for medical school with a prayer on the last day possible to gain acceptance for the class of 1962. Another amazing thing occurred—I was accepted! I am sure I was number 150 of the class of 150 accepted at the University of Texas Medical Branch for 1962. An interesting note is that of the 150 students accepted, there were 147 men and only 3 women in my class! In those days, men dominated medical school classes. I started medical school in Galveston Texas around September 1, 1962, and Pam reentered the University of Texas in Austin.

Pam had decided not to go to medical school and that I would be the only doctor in the family. She was determined to graduate on time and was able to convince the chairman of the Department of Psychology to allow her to take the entire four-year degree program in psychology in a single year! Those of you who remember Pam will realize this was a minor challenge for her. We would be apart for most of the time during the next year. It turns out, however, that I spent every weekend of my freshman year at Galveston going to Austin to visit Pam and her family. The only weekends I spent in Galveston were the weekends before major exams. I studied hard Monday through Thursday and would leave immediately following class on Friday to drive to Austin. Everybody knew I would be leaving at 5:00 p.m. Friday and if they wanted a ride to Austin, they had better be there on time. I would return on Sunday night, usually in a panic that I had not been studying, and would study some Sunday night and diligently on Monday through Thursday. Pam graduated on time and was able to get an "emergency" teaching certificate. She taught chemistry and physics at the Ursuline Academy in Galveston during my second year of medical school. She had an apartment at the other end of Galveston Island. We saw each other on a daily basis that second year.

CHAPTER 5

The Medical School Years

I remember the drive from Austin to Galveston to start medical school and crossing the causeway bridge to Galveston in my 1959 Ford Fairlane with the Thunderbird engine. I wondered what the future would hold and, frankly, was quite frightened. It turned out that a high school friend, Johnny Webb, was in my freshman class. We became roommates. We both pledged the medical fraternity Nu Sigma Nu and lived at the fraternity house. I remember walking to school the first day. Johnny and I had walked to the old medical school building ("Big Red") to get some things at the bookstore. Walking across the street from "Big Red" to the Anatomy building for our first lecture in medical school, I was very nervous. I said a quick prayer for God's help.

Back in our room that afternoon, Johnny introduced me to one of his friends, Jack Henry, who was starting his junior year of medical school. Jack became a good friend, and both he and Johnny were in our wedding two years later. That afternoon, Jack made a recommendation that change my life. Was it another coincidence or the hand of God? He suggested I go to one of the medical school professors and volunteer to do "whatever" to help the professor in a research project. He recommended

I meet the new, young professor that had just returned from Johns Hopkins infectious disease program. I started as a medical student research assistant for Dr. John Perry shortly after that.

While I was in my sophomore year in medical school, Pam was working at Ursuline Academy, an all-girls school, teaching chemistry and physics to high school students. During that year, President John F. Kennedy was assassinated (November 22, 1963). I remember walking through the halls of John Sealy Hospital on my way to take an examination in Psychiatry. Everyone was listening to their radios and televisions regarding the event. I asked several people what happened and learning that Pres. Kennedy had been shot. We all entered the room where the examination was being given. As I recall, the chief of Psychiatry walked in the room and threw the examination on the desk. He said, "A crazy man has just shot our president. If you want to take this examination, it's okay. It's also okay if you don't take the examination. I'm going home." We all left the examination on the desk and went home to find out what was happening. Pam and I spent the next few days watching the TV regarding the events of that November 1963.

Dr. Perry was pleased with my work and recommended that I continue my research at Johns Hopkins. I was working on a project related to gram-negative septicemia with associated adrenal hemorrhage. Dr. Perry arranged for me to have a six-month research sabbatical from medical school with his prior chief of infectious diseases at Johns Hopkins Hospital, Dr. Leighton Cluff. Pam and I decided that this six-month period between my sophomore and junior years of medical school would be a good time to get married. I did have to take a few courses at Johns Hopkins medical school to keep up with my class, so I took Dermatology and Ophthalmology while I was there.

I finished my sophomore year final exams somewhere around April 8, 1964. I drove to Austin to prepare for our wedding. The rehearsal dinner was on April 10, and the wedding was at St. Austin's Catholic Church in Austin, Texas, on April 11. Another miracle occurred—I married Pam King.

Pam and I had to pack my little Nash Rambler (a small car that is no longer made) with enough stuff to live in Baltimore, Maryland, for six months! We left for Johns Hopkins immediately following the reception for our wedding. Our best man, Johnny Webb, had cleverly hidden our car so that there were no paintings or tin cans to worry about on our long drive.

With the help of God, Pam and I had remained virgins during the five years prior to marriage. Since we did not feel birth control was right, we had to wait even longer before the marriage was consummated. According to the "rhythm system" of birth control, we were unable to have relations until we had reached Washington DC five days later! We offered up this time for a perfect marriage. Pam and I were convinced that our oldest son, Trey, was conceived the first time we had relations (another miracle). Although very surprised, we were extremely happy that our planned birth control had failed.

During the first part of her pregnancy, Pam had a lot of morning sickness. Each morning I would wake up and take my INH and vitamins for the TB skin test conversion. The smell from the pills would make her vomit. There was a time that the only thing she could eat was watermelon. Fortunately, she loved watermelon. One day I had purchased a beautiful watermelon, cut it in half, and placed it our icebox. The next morning, I noticed the entire heart of both halves of the watermelon had been eaten completely. I asked her what had happened. She said a mouse must have gotten in the refrigerator. I explained that it must've been a "mama mouse." After that, Pamela was frequently referred to as "Mama Mouse." Because of that event and the story related to it, a dear friend of ours later wrote a story using oil paintings on small pieces of canvas that became the famous "mouse book." It has subsequently vanished; I hope one of the children has it somewhere.

Baltimore was very hot. Our apartment had windows on only one side with no cross ventilation. We were not sure we would survive the summer. One of Pam's professors from the University of Texas (Lois Chatham) had moved to Washington DC. While visiting her one weekend, Lois and George provided us with a window air conditioner that we placed in our bedroom. Thanks to the Chathams, we survive that summer. George had an important job at the Library of Congress. We had many amazing intellectual conversations with that wonderful couple. They provided us with a "family" for our first trip away from home. Thank you, Jesus, for that relationship.

That fall we returned to Galveston to start my junior year. We continue to be blessed. Our first son was born on January 8, 1965. At the end of my junior year, I was accepted into the Alpha Omega

Alpha honor medical society as vice president. That meant that my medical school standing was number 2 in the class of 150. A miracle for sure!

Early during the senior year, we had to make arrangements for applications for internship. In those days, the first year out of medical school was referred to as internship. The Vietnam War was also heating up, and all physicians had to make some type of arrangement or be drafted as a general medical officer. The joke was "If you could hear thunder and see lightning and were a physician, you'd be going into the army." Arrangements had to be made for some type of government service. I applied for the National Institutes of Health (Public Health Service) and the air force's Berry Plan. The Berry Plan was a type of draft deferment that would allow you to finish your postdoctoral training and enter the military as a specialist rather than be drafted as a general medical officer. I was accepted to be deferred with the Berry Plan and, upon completion, would be eligible to enter the air force as an internal medicine physician. I was still hoping, however, for the NIH appointment.

My time with Dr. Perry and at Johns Hopkins had led me to the decision that I wanted to go into internal medicine. I applied to Texas Southwestern Medical School in Dallas, Johns Hopkins Hospital, University of Texas Galveston, Washington University St. Louis, Yale, Harvard Mass General, and Harvard Boston City. My internship would begin July 1,1966.

We were one of the first classes to use the "matching program." This program allowed each intern applicant to list the hospitals in the order of his or her preference. Each of the hospitals would list their candidates in the order of their preference. A computer would select the best match. The two places I wanted to go to were the Harvard hospitals in Boston. Because of my inferiority complex, I listed them next to last, feeling comfortable that all the others would accept me. I was fearful of competing with the Ivy League elite. Pam and I sent the list to the matching program with a prayer that God would send me to the place He felt was best for me. The prayer lifted up as we dropped the application in the mailbox was *"Thy will be done."* As it turned out, another amazing thing occurred. Harvard Boston City Hospital Service was listed fourth or fifth on my list. I was excited but, frankly, quite frightened when I open my letter and found I had been accepted to the intern class July 1966 at the Harvard II-IV Medical Service at Boston City Hospital! This truly was a miracle, since I was turned down by all the places where I'd felt sure I would be accepted! In retrospect, this miracle changed my life forever.

On January 8, 1965, Trey was born by C-section at Galveston John Sealy Hospital. I was on the OB-GYN pediatric service rotation of my junior year.

One night while studying during my junior year, I kept thinking of one of our friends in Baltimore, Maryland, whom we had met while we were living on Conant Way. Pam had not learned to cook for only two people, so we often had our friends over for dinner. This habit became part of life. A frequent companion at the table, Pam and I had gotten to know Frank Sullivan well during our six months in Baltimore. That particular night I had a great deal of trouble studying and kept thinking about Frank.

I finally got up and went into our bedroom to visit with Pam. I told her my thoughts of Frank. She was amazed! She had been thinking about him quite intensely for the past hour as well. We both thought this was rather strange and tried to call Frank. We were unable to reach him but reached one of our other friends. We learned that Frank had been killed in a car accident that day. This episode taught me a lesson that has stayed with me all my life: *stay in touch with your feelings*. If your feelings are good and holy, act on them.

I graduated with high honors from the University of Texas Medical Branch in June 1966. Amazing grace! I took my medical board examination in Fort Worth, Texas, for my Texas license to practice medicine. I left Pam and Trey with her parents (Bommie and Boppie, as Trey had named them). After taking the exam, I drove to Boston, Massachusetts, by myself. On the way to Boston, I stopped at the National Institutes of Health for an interview. I hoped that I would be accepted to do research there for my two required years of service to our country. The National Institutes of Health was part of the Public Health Service and would count as military duty if accepted. That interview made me a day late starting my internship in Boston. At the time, I didn't realize what a great mistake that was!

CHAPTER 6

Internship Residency Training

When I arrived at BCH (Boston City Hospital), it was the night of the first day of my internship, July 1, 1966. I called my resident in charge and was greeted by an angry young physician who would be my medical leader for the next couple of months. He griped at me all the way to the medical officer building where I would spend the next three months of my life. He informed me that it was totally unacceptable to be late or skip a day and that it should never happen again! I spent the next three months on the all-male medical ward on the fifth floor of the medical building at BCH. The following morning was my first day as an intern at BCH. Forty-nine years later, I can still clearly remember that day. I was, frankly, scared to death. I spent a lot of time in the bathroom with "emotional diarrhea." I will never forget the first time a Harvard medical student handed me an order to countersign as the medical intern in charge of that patient. This was quite a traumatic and scary event that reinforced that I was actually in charge of the patient's life. I said to myself, *"It begins. God help me!"*!

Not only did I have the stress of beginning a new career under the direction of the resident with whom I had already had an unpleasant encounter, I was without my wife and child. They were the source of my happiness. Since I had not found a place to live in Boston, Pam and Trey were still in Texas. Each day I would "go home" to the medical officer building, where I would spend the night after eating at the hospital. I had the stress of finding a new apartment in the big city of Boston, Massachusetts. In those days there was no such things as text messaging or e-mail. The only communication was by letter, since we had no money to call by telephone. My first year out of medical school would generate a grand total of $3600 for the entire year! Yes, that's right, only $300 a month before taxes for twelve months! Pam had been a schoolteacher in Galveston and had been making around $5000 a year. She could not obtain a teacher certificate in Massachusetts and, therefore, we were living on poverty wages. If it was not for Bommie, Boppie, and my father, we would have all starved to death I'm sure. There were many episodes that occurred during my years at BCH. I will relate a few of them in this book. These episodes started to shape my feelings that ultimately helped me see the problems in health care delivery in these United States.

One patient that I remember was admitted with pneumonia and liver problems. He was an alcoholic. My resident on evening rounds made the comment, "You better restrain him before he goes into the DTs tonight." I was horrified at the idea of restraining someone and said I would watch him closely. We always made late-night rounds usually around eleven o'clock. I was using a flashlight to read the bedside chart. When I turn on the flashlight to look at this patient's bed-side chart, he jumped out of bed and landed on top of me. He was having some horrible delusion and felt I was some creature. The ward clerk and one of my fellow interns rescued me. After a huge struggle with a totally disorientated patient, we finally got him restrained. He was thoroughly confused in his delirium tremens. On rounds the next morning, my resident leader smiled and said, "Next time, you better listen to me."

I chose internal medicine over pediatrics reasoning that I would have more conversations with my patients who were adult and could speak. At BCH, however, a huge number of patients were alcoholics, many of whom were admitted totally confused and unable to provide an adequate history. I remember another episode with an alcoholic admitted with total confusion related to Korsakoff's psychosis. He was pleasantly demented and would answer whatever question asked with whatever came into his mind at the time. Confabulation is a part of this syndrome, and he demonstrated that freely. He tended to wander through the ward at night. He was always looking for a card game. On one occasion, I heard shrieks from the ladies on the floor above us. The sixth medical floor was an all-ladies ward. There was no air conditioning at the BCH, and in the summertime all the windows were open, making it easy to hear the screaming from the floor above us. We looked and Benny (an alias) was gone from his bed. We ran up the stairs to the sixth floor and found Benny waking up one of the sleeping woman, asking her where the card game was. He was half-naked with his hospital gown flapping in the breeze! You can imagine all the women in this open floor ward shrieking with horror at a half-naked, confused man on their all-woman floor. We guided Benny back to our floor.

On another occasion, Benny wandered up two or possibly three floors, I can't remember, to the neurosurgical operating room. Again the windows were open, and we could hear extensive screaming and cursing from the neurosurgeon in the middle of the night. The neurosurgical resident was performing a burr hole surgery on a patient with a subdural hematoma. Everyone was apparently so busy that they hadn't noticed Benny walking into the operating room. He walked up behind the neurosurgeon right as the neurosurgeon was preparing to drill the burr hole. Benny tapped him on the shoulder and asked, "Where's the game?" You can imagine the excitement that this generated in the neurosurgical operating room. We again retrieved Benny and restrained him. He was like Houdini and could escape from any type of restraint.

I remember one episode where I was so tired, having been up for almost forty-eight hours straight, that I fell asleep standing up. We were frequently up all night and many nights had only two to four hours of sleep. We considered any sleep a good night. As interns, we have to not only take care of the patients—such as completing a history physical as well as daily follow-up on each of our patients—we also had many other chores. We started all the IVs, put down all the nasogastric tubes, drew all the blood tests, did the blood counts, looked at all blood smears to see the types of cells present, and completed the urinalysis and microscopic urine sediments. All of these things had to be entered by hand in the patient's chart before morning rounds with our attending physician. We also had to spin down the blood and separate the serum from the formed elements for blood chemistries. The lab at BCH would not accept anything but the separated serum.

When I tell people these things they find it hard to believe, but that's the way it was in 1966 at the BCH.

One of our attending physicians was a famous infectious disease specialist, who was gifted in everything except speaking to residents. He would look at the ground and speak in a monotone, which tended to put one to sleep. Although he always said amazing things and taught us a lot, his speaking delivery was lacking. One day on attending rounds, as we called it, his voice hummed me to sleep while I was standing at the bedside with him and two of my intern colleagues. Since this professor always spoke while looking at the ground and was short in stature, he did not notice that I had fallen asleep standing up! My fellow interns noticed and wedged me between their bodies so the three of us remained vertical as a single phalanx while I slept. It reminds me of the words of the song "He Ain't Heavy, He's My Brother." We all felt like brothers of an army company under fire. Our training in many respects was like Army Ranger training. You were pushed to the brink of exhaustion and were expected to think quickly and correctly whenever the occasion arose. The sixteen of us in that internship class were like soldiers under fire, and we helped each other survive the fire-fight.

One of the two interns holding me up was my dear friend Charlie Hatem, a Harvard Medical School graduate. I remember when I first met him. On that day, I was accepting patients who were being admitted from the clinic to our ward. Charlie arrived with his patient in a wheelchair. He had brought the patient to our floor from the clinic building himself. His presentation of the patient's problem was very clear and concise, and I was totally amazed. I thought he must be one of the senior residents, but it turned out he was one of my fellow interns. Charlie never ceased to amaze me with his intelligence, caring of patients, and humor. All these traits were necessary to survive the BCH. I learned a lot from Charlie.

In September 1966, Pam and Trey moved to the apartment I'd found in Brookline, Massachusetts. I would come home totally exhausted around nine or ten o'clock on my night off, often after being gone for two days. Pam would keep Trey up so that he would know his father. One of Trey's first sentences was, "Here's Johnny." For some of you young folks reading this, you may not remember that's how Johnny Carson started his late-night TV show at ten o'clock EST. I remember frequently falling asleep with my face in my food. Pam would help me up and put me in bed. I would get up at six o'clock the next morning and go back for another one to two days on the ward without coming home. We all worked so hard that it was unthinkable to miss a day of work. I remember going to work with a fever of 104 on one occasion and with a gastrointestinal virus with vomiting on another occasion. All of my fellow interns followed the same procedure, and I don't remember anybody missing a day of work that year.

I finally finished the first three months on the ward, and I was planning for a two-week vacation back to Texas. Pam and Trey were to meet me when I was supposed to finish the night's work, around ten o'clock in the morning. There was so much work to do that by two in the afternoon I was getting very upset knowing that Pam and Trey had been waiting for me three to four hours in the hospital parking lot. My vacation had actually started earlier that morning! There was a very sick person that I was taking care of and I carefully told the intern who was taking my place what the problem was and what I was doing to take care of the problem. There were, of course, many other patients that I transferred to his care at that meeting. The new intern taking my place understood all the problems, but this one was critical.

I reached the car totally exhausted and drained, both mentally and physically. I crawled into the back of our station wagon and went to sleep. I think I slept there for approximately ten hours. Pam and Trey had driven through the night. Sometime in the early morning hours, I was awakened by a great racket coming from the top of the car. I looked out the back window of our station wagon in time to see our bags flying off the roof of the car, landing on the highway, and breaking open with clothes going down the side of the mountain. To give me a place to sleep, I had placed our bags in the luggage rack but had not secure them very well. Pam and I both collected our clothes off a Virginia hillside, repacked the bags, and continued our journey. We drove straight through to Texas. In those days, it took about thirty-six hours. We had a great vacation and did not think about leaving until the Friday before I had to be back at work the following Monday. We, therefore, had to drive straight through going back to get to Boston on time!

As we reached New England on the returning trip, all the leaves had fallen off the trees. It was a very gray day. I member the feeling of depression and dread as we returned to Boston. I realized I would be back on a busy schedule and not see Pamela and Trey very much for the remainder of my internship year (another eight to nine months). On arriving back at BCH, my resident, who had given me such a hard time when arriving one day late at the start of the internship, blamed me for the death of the patient I'd left the first day of my vacation. I was told I should not have left a sick patient until he was healthy enough to survive without my care. It didn't make any difference that I had transferred all information to a very bright fellow intern. That episode has haunted me all my life. It was tough in the first few months as a doctor to be blamed for the death of one of my patients. Many years later I did a radio show with my good friend Charlie Hatem, and we discussed this point. Charlie, after hearing the story, felt I was not the blame for the patient's death. The patient had a critical illness and would've died no matter who was taking care of him. He was very upset that this resident had blamed me and felt sorry that I have suffered through the years because of that event. That helped me a lot, but certainly the episode had shaped my feelings for the remainder of my career. I was always fearful when I would need to leave. Passing on the care of a patient to one of my colleagues, for whatever reason, remained a traumatic event and always a difficult situation. I had always been compulsive, but this episode made me even more compulsive about dealing with patient care. I have learned that Jesus is a very forgiving person, even if my resident was not. My loving family always understood my many absences from family events that this compulsion caused.

There was a Catholic church across the street from the BCH. In those days, there were no "beepers" or mobile phones that allowed a physician to be reached when off the floor. On the days I was on call, I spent the night in the hospital in the medical officers building. To go the church when on call on Sundays, I would check out with my resident so he could cover my patients while I walk across the street to go to church. Our uniform as interns was a white smock with a mandarin collar. I was easily recognized as an intern at the BCH. I would routinely fall asleep in the pew during the Mass. One of the priests became very familiar with me doing this. When Mass was over and everyone was out of the church, he would come to me and in the loving voice say, "It's okay, son. God knows you need your sleep. It's time to go back to work."

The hospital provided free food for the interns and residents. There were four meals a day. The cafeteria would be open for exactly one hour. If you did not make it through the door on time, it was locked and you went without a meal. Since there were no beepers or cell phones, if we were needed, the phone at the front would ring and our stomachs would turn over thinking we might be the one they were looking for. Frequently emergencies would happen during meals, which became a pattern for the rest of my life. When I heard the call "Dr. Cashion, you are needed on the floor," I would leave my food and run to the fifth or sixth floor where the Harvard II medical patients were located. The elevators at BCH were very slow and unsure. Therefore, that meant we had to run up the five flights of stairs to the medical floor. Arriving breathless, we frequently faced some medical crisis that required clear thinking and urgent attention. The adrenaline in those situations made us forget our hunger and our drowsiness. Fellow interns would often gather up some food in a napkin since there were no stores in that area of Boston where you could even buy a hot dog. These episodes resulted in developing a habit of eating very fast. The minute food was in front of you, you would inhale it as fast as possible in fear that the phone would ring and you would not get to eat. That habit has persisted all these years, and I still eat too fast.

At the BCH, the Harvard interns made all the final decisions. Of course there was outstanding help from our residents and stellar attending physicians. They made sure we didn't do anything wrong, but the decision was always left to the intern. There was a cardiologist who was head of the Harvard Cardiology program at the BCH. He was well known and respected throughout the world for his research and clinical acumen. He was doing a study to question the then-respected policy of three weeks of bed rest required for patients with a myocardial infarction (heart attack). The protocol for the research required taking a person who had been on bed rest for three weeks following their myocardial infarction and putting them on a tilt table to monitor what happened when they were first ambulated. This is a classic study and published in the *New England Journal of Medicine* sometime around 1967. This was a classic study and proved that early ambulation was a better approach for people with myocardial infarction rather than the three weeks of bed rest practiced at that time. We of course did not know the outcome of the study in 1966.

I remember a sweet lady who had been admitted to my service with an acute myocardial infarction. In those days, medication was the only option for treatment of myocardial infarction. Cardiac intervention did not exist. I really became close to her during the three weeks of her bed rest and loved her as I loved all my patients. The staff cardiologist wanted to use her in this landmark study. My good friend Charlie Hatem had had a patient the week before who had almost died on the tilt table. I knew the details of the story since Charlie and I were so close, I did not want my patient to be part of the study.

I remember the very angry staff cardiologist with his red face screaming with his Germanic accent at me, "How can a lowly intern prevent a Harvard professor from completing his research study?" I simply stated, "She is my patient, and I don't want her to go through the procedure." Of course this decision reached the highest levels of our Harvard group at BCH. The chief of service told the cardiologist, "Interns have the final decision in this training program." *My decision stood, but I'm not sure how tall!* Two years later, when I was applying for cardiology fellowships, I was fearful that I would be eliminated from all programs because of this decision.

While an intern at the BCH, I participated in the "Boston Heal-In." This was an event organized by Phil Caper and several other resident physicians at the BCH. Phil was an assistant resident while I was an intern on the Harvard II-IV Medical Service. Phil was one of the resident leaders who was very interested in raising our salary from poverty wages and improving the working hours we all suffered with. The *Boston Globe* had published a human interest story stating that doctors in training in Boston had to sell their blood to feed their children. In those days, a person could donate blood and be paid for it. Phil was able to work with the Boston University and Tufts residents to organize and coordinate efforts for a successful "reverse strike."

The City of Boston had refused to raise intern/resident salaries and reduce the long working hours. My intern salary was $3600 for one year of working, just $300 a month before taxes. Phil and the other two medical school residency programs had been unsuccessful in petitioning the City of Boston for increased salaries and better working hours.

It was decided we had to strike! It would be a reverse strike. We would take care of our patients as if we were a private hospital. At that time, Boston City Hospital was around fifteen hundred beds, as I recall. Prior to the strike, there was a policy agreed to by all residents to keep the residents from being overloaded. It was generally agreed upon that the patients needed to be near death with multiple medical problems before they were admitted. The less sick were followed as outpatients. With that philosophy, the Boston City Hospital ran about 75 to 80 percent occupancy. The City of Boston had budgeted for around 80 percent occupancy. It is interesting that in those days not many things were done as an outpatient. Outpatient medicine has become a way of life in today's practice. This was not the case in 1967.

The plan for the "Heal-In" was to admit patients with less severe illnesses who normally would have been admitted to private hospitals but at that time not to the Boston City Hospital. Doing this we could keep the hospital at 100 percent occupancy and "bust" the city budget.

It took a great deal of effort from the three medical school residency programs to supply continuous good medical care despite the increased workload. The resident leaders from the three medical school were able to pull it off. As an intern, my part was to work day and night until the strike was over. We all work hard and even longer hours than normal to be sure no patient suffered. In fact, patients receive better care than many would have, since the extra patients would have been sent home as outpatients rather than admitted.

After approximately one week, the City of Boston caved in to the request. Intern salaries were raised from $3600 to, as I recall, $5000 a year. This led to better "house staff" wages across the United States. It was probably the start of the medical education revolution that ultimately led to better hours and a better salary.

There are many other amazing stories that I will share with you. However, I am drawn back to the purpose of this book: to show the influence of God in my life and how I have arrived at a concept to change the delivery of medical care. I must stay on track and remind you to look to how God has shaped my life. It was the grace of God that allowed me to survive that year as an intern. It was an amazing year, with my medical knowledge growing at an exponential rate. I can remember starting my second year of training. In those days it was referred to as the junior assistant resident year, a.k.a. the "JAR year."

I learned many things on the II-IV Harvard Medical Service. One of the important things that would influence my life and some of my beliefs about medical care in the USA I learned from dealing with patients who were in absolute poverty with no family or insurance backup. When I returned to celebrate my fortieth anniversary as chief resident on the II-IV Harvard Service, there was a phrase used by one of my contemporaries. It involved dealing with the "pathos of poverty." I cannot remember who made that statement, but it profoundly covered our education at the Boston City Hospital. These experiences helped me form a concept of medical care that I will discuss later.

I started my second year of postdoctoral residency training in July 1967. We were junior assistant residents (JARs). I started that year working at one of the outlying Harvard hospitals. The Mount Auburn Hospital was a dramatic change from the BCH. It was a hospital with mostly private patients. It was a beautiful community hospital with outstanding service and an outstanding reputation. "The Mount," as it was called, had its own intern program. The Harvard medical residents from BCH supervised those interns. We were not up all night, at least not as much as the prior year. We were able to have a little more time at home. As I remember, but I'm not certain, I think it was the year the Boston Red Sox did well in the playoffs and the song "Impossible Dream" was popular. I felt I was living the impossible dream. With God's grace, the boy who was not supposed to have made it through college much less medical school was a resident at the prestigious Harvard Medical Service. That represents part of the amazing grace God granted in my life.

During this year, Pam became very ill and almost died. I remember hearing her weak little voice on the telephone calling for help. I left the hospital immediately and drove home. We left Trey with some good friends and neighbors. I drove Pam to the Mount Auburn Hospital. She was very sick with a high fever and dehydration. It turned out to be urosepsis. She was so sick that everybody was having difficulty starting an IV on her. In those days, central lines did not exist. Pam was laying in the bed and pleading with me to start her IV since nobody else could accomplish this necessary treatment task. With the help of God, I was able to start it the first time. She always remembered that and would frequently tell people, "If you ever need an IV started, get Dick to do it." I don't think she or I realized that was more of God's grace. This occurred early in my career, before I realized the influence of God in my life and how many miracles went unrecognized. It is amazing what you can discover when you review each day to find the many miracles that could otherwise go unrecognized. I now realize it was not me but rather Jesus working through me that accomplished the task of starting Pam's IV and many other things that occurred in those years. At that time in my life, I took credit for the accomplishments and did not claim my dependence on Jesus to accomplish these things. It was many years later before I understood this fact.

Pam recovered after approximately a week in the hospital. Because of my job at the hospital and Pam's absence, Trey would hardly let Pam out of his sight the next many years. Trey had stayed with our dear friends and neighbors from Mexico, Sandy and Philipe Ochoa. The couple had a little girl names Alexandra, pronounced the Spanish way. She was Trey's age. We all became great friends. *Thank you, Jesus.*

In the spring of 1968, toward the end of my JAR year, I was on the Harvard Neurologic Service at the BCH under the direction of Dr. Denny-Brown. It was a very enjoyable rotation except for the stress of presenting cases to Dr. Denny-Brown, which was always a traumatic event.

Pam was pregnant for the second time. She was in her "nesting phase." She felt that Trey and I should go fishing on the afternoon of May 5, 1968. It was a beautiful day. It was a Sunday and I was not on call. She stayed at home and we went to a small lake in Brookline, Massachusetts. In those days, you could rent little rowboats on that lake. We had a great day fishing—not catching many fish, but it was great to be together and outside. On our return home, I found Sandy in our apartment in a panic. She had been worried that I would come home and find Pam gone. Pam's water had broken, and she had gone into labor. Sandy's husband, Philippe, had been instructed to take Pam to the hospital. Later I received the heroic story about Philippe driving Pam to the hospital in his little Volkswagen, swerving around obstacles and driving well over the speed limit. He related to me that he was totally terrified by the thought of Pam delivering in his little car with him in attendance. This fear allowed him to drive at amazing speeds through the Boston traffic to arrive at Boston Lying Inn Hospital.

Pam related her version of the story of Philippe's wild drive to the hospital. She remembers him driving very fast, swerving in and out of traffic, honking his horn, and speaking a lot of Spanish words that were probably both profanities and prayers. He related the story of being confronted by the nurses to gain medical information about Pam. All he could say was "I'm not the husband!" By the time I arrived at the hospital, Jarrod had already been delivered by cesarean section (Pam's second

C-section). Later that afternoon, I brought Trey to the hospital to visit his mother and brother. The hospital would not allow Trey to come and visit Pam. I remember taking Trey to a spot where he could see Pam. She was in a second or third story window and waving to us. Trey was very cute with his little beanie hat with a propeller on top. Bommie was already on an airplane to come and rescue us, since I would have to go back to work on Monday. Doctors in training and fathers in general at that time were not allowed to take off time from work to be with their wife and newborn children. We were now a family of four.

Dr. Dwight Harkin was a heart surgeon at the Brigham Hospital in Boston. He had done some of the world's first open-heart surgeries and was a well-known Harvard surgeon. He also did heart surgery at the Mount Auburn Hospital. One episode I remember while I was a resident at Mount Auburn was an encounter with Dr. Harkin. He did not want any of the medical residents to deal with his patients, since he had surgical fellows that were at the hospital full-time. On one occasion, however, I walked into the ICU and found Dr. Harkin holding down a patient who had just had heart surgery and was on a ventilator. He was having a grand mal seizure. Dr. Harkin's surgical fellows were not available. I went up and tapped him on the shoulder and asked if I could help. He screamed some profanity, which I interpreted as yes. Valium had recently been released, and I knew it would stop seizures. I ordered the nurse to obtain some IV Valium. I gave the Valium intravenously, and the patient's seizures stopped immediately. Dr. Harkin jumped up and said, "What was that!" From that time on, Dr. Harken would allow us to take care of immediate problems when his fellow was not available.

While I was working at the Mount Auburn Hospital, Bobby Kennedy was shot. I remember our sadness on that day. It was June 6, 1968, the day that Robert Kennedy was assassinated. I remember all the turmoil and questions regarding what was going on following the second Kennedy assassination.

That rotation was my last rotation of my junior assistant residency year. By the end of the JAR year, I had decided on my future postdoctoral training. I had already been accepted as a senior resident on the Harvard Medical Service, a position that would run from July 1968 through July 1969. I had always planned to go into infectious diseases, considering my past research at Johns Hopkins Hospital and the University of Texas Medical Branch. During my residency, however, I noticed cardiac problems were particularly interesting to me—especially the urgent ones that occurred in the middle of night. I had gradually changed my mind and decided to go into cardiology.

Cardiology fellowship training programs were extremely competitive. Candidates were required to apply to these positions a year and a half or two years ahead of time. At the time, Dr. Proctor Harvey at Georgetown University Hospital had developed one of the leading clinical cardiology programs. One of the residents—John Abrams, who was a year ahead of me—had gone to this program and was very happy there. I decided I didn't have a chance at any of the Harvard programs because of my prior encounter with the chief of cardiology at the BCH. I was also most interested in becoming a practicing clinical cardiologist. Dr. Harvey's program was the best for that.

The Road From Troas

The acting director of our internal medicine program at the BCH was Dr. Charles Davidson. He spent a lot of time with each of the residents in planning their future education. I had my routine meetings with him to discuss future plans and told him that I had change my mind about going into infectious diseases. I can remember Dr. Davidson's comment: "There is nothing new in cardiology. You need to go into immunology or pulmonary diseases. Why not continue your work in infectious diseases?" He made the comment that we were replacing heart valves, had digitalis, mercurial diuretics, and nitroglycerin. "What else is there to do in cardiology?" My comment was, "I do not know, but I just find great excitement and interest in dealing with cardiac emergencies. If I'm going to be up all night dealing with sick patients, why not pick something that I truly love?" The adrenaline rush in fighting a cardiac emergency stimulated my brain. This was particularly helpful when these episodes occurred in the middle of night. I found I would think very clearly and do the right thing, even when exhausted. At the time, I credited myself with the ability to deal with these emergencies, but in retrospect I realize it was the Holy Spirit. Anyway, I wanted to be a cardiologist. Many years later, while I was in Houston practicing "the dead specialty," as Dr. Davidson had called it, I would talk with Dr. Davidson and tease him about all the things that had happened in cardiology since I had left the BCH. In fact, I was really enjoying "practicing the dead specialty" at the Houston Medical Center with Drs. DeBakey and Cooley.

CHAPTER 7

Cardiology Fellowship

I was accepted as a cardiology fellow at Georgetown University Hospital in the program directed by Dr. Proctor Harvey. More amazing grace! At that time this program was felt to be one of the very best clinical cardiology programs in the United States. I began my fellowship July 1969 on the Georgetown Medical Service at DC General Hospital with Dr. Ross Fletcher. I was making rounds with Ross Fletcher in the Intensive Care unit at DC General Hospital on July 16, 1969, when Neil Armstrong took his "one small step for man, one giant leap for mankind." I had taken a giant step in starting my cardiology fellowship. During that rotation, there were many demonstrations against the Vietnam War. There were so many arrests they had to develop a "tent jail" on the grounds of DC General Hospital. It was quite a scene.

Over the next two years, I would rotate through DC General Hospital, Georgetown University Hospital, National Institutes of Health, and the Armed Forces Institute of Pathology. As fellows in cardiology, we were on call for the entire time on each rotation—yes every night and weekend. However, as a consulting service we rarely had to go in at night. Once we finished our work, we could head home to be with our families. Pam and I really enjoyed living in Washington DC. I was making a grand total of $6000 a year and, therefore, had to find means of making extra money. Bommie, Boppie, and my father all continued to help. Moonlighting, as it was called when a physician in training worked elsewhere for money, was not allowed but necessary. Pam and I drove all over Washington DC doing insurance physicals. One of the cardiology staff, who I met while at DC General, became a good friend, and we actually developed a nighttime practice in his office. He hired us to cover his nighttime clinic. That helped a lot.

I was lucky, and we had our first vacation during my first year as a cardiology fellow in November 1969. We were able to return to Texas for Thanksgiving. I don't remember exactly how it happened, but we were able to fly home for that Thanksgiving. I'll bet Boppie paid for the tickets. Pam was pregnant for the third time. Our vacation was spent mostly in the family home on Inks Lake. I was able to moonlight in Burnet, Texas, for the primary care physicians there who loved to go hunting during that season. I remember an incident resulting in my urgent callback to the Burnet Hospital. A car wreck had occurred, and a young teenage boy was severely injured. It was obvious on my evaluation that he was in shock, probably from a ruptured spleen. I called the primary care doctors back. They had learned surgery "on the front lines of medicine in rural Texas." It was unlikely this boy would survive an ambulance drive to Austin (no helicopter transfer in those days); this boy was too sick. We went straight to the operating room. I was totally amazed at their surgical skills. Post-op the boy was very sick and complicated. I spent the next several days and nights at his bedside in the ICU in this tiny little hospital. Considering his multiple injuries, it was truly a miracle that he survived and left the hospital. More amazing grace in my life!

At the end of our two weeks, it was time to head back to Washington DC. We were packing at the home on Inks Lake. Pam went into her nesting phase, as she called it. She began having rhythmic back pains consistent with her prior labor pains. Pam was headed to her third C-section. She was only six months pregnant at the time. We packed up, jumped in the car, and drove to Austin, Texas, where I had arranged for her to see an OB-GYN doctor. His name was Dr. Derossier (can't remember how it was spelled). He was our sister-in-law's doctor (Rowdy's wife).

He confirmed that Pam was in labor. He was very concerned considering her two prior C-sections and felt the best course of action was for Pam to have a normal delivery. He believed the baby would have less chance of developing a severe lung disease like the one that had killed one of President Kennedy's newborns. She was in labor all day November 29, 1969. At around midnight, Pam was going to have our third child. The actual delivery occurred at midnight. Pam and I were asked what day we wanted on the birth certificate since our third son was born exactly at midnight. Did we want 11/29 or 11/30. Pam said it should be November 29 since she had been in labor all that day and he was delivered at midnight. Our third son was very small. I don't remember the exact weight, but it was around three pounds. He was placed in the ICU at Breckenridge Hospital and lived there for the next two months. He was baptized twice, even though that is not church policy, by Father Matoka, who had performed the marriage ceremony for Pam and I and had baptized Trey. He came to the hospital for the baptism. (Jarrod had been baptized in Boston.) Pam wanted a formal baptismal ceremony for this third son and, as I recall, Father allowed it to happen later. I had to return to Washington DC to go back to work. Pam stayed with Trey and Jarrod at Bommie and Boppie's house. Hade lived in the neonatal ICD at Breckenridge Hospital. We were all finally reunited two months later. I was allowed to take off work to fly with them back to Washington. Boppie also paid for those tickets.

One interesting event occurred during my first year of cardiology training at Georgetown University Hospital. One of the greatest parts of that training was being able to be close to Dr. Proctor Harvey. Many people feel he was one of the greatest teachers of clinical cardiology. I feel he was the best! One of the rotations with Dr. Harvey included being responsible for his famous Thursday night teaching conference. His weekly teaching conferences were so great that at least fifty private physicians from the Washington DC area would come each week. Dr. Harvey had the first auditorium with stephophones (electronic stethoscopes), so everyone in the audience could listen to the patient's heart sounds with Dr. Harvey. He was great at mimicking heart sounds and murmurs. He would describe what we should hear by mimicking the sounds for emphasis. His teaching was so famous that someone decided to film a series of these conferences and allow physicians to watch them at home on television. A TV film crew came and began the filming. I was the fellow responsible for getting all the things ready for Dr. Harvey to perform his magical teaching on television. This was one of the first real breakthroughs in teaching physicians at home. It was 1969. We were taught the art of auscultation of the heart better than anyone.

All was ready for the television production. We were all wearing pale blue/green rather than white coats so the light reflection would not "blind" the camera. That conference went great except for one thing. Everyone in the auditorium could hear Dr. Harvey and the heart sounds; however, *someone* didn't have the correct sound connection feeding the TV recordings. No one knew about the problem until the program was reviewed several days later. We all learned the correct connections so no more mistakes would occur, and the remainder of the series went off without a hitch.

The TV engineers fell in love with Dr. Harvey's delightful southern gentleman's personality. During this time, Dr. Harvey was elected to president of the national American Heart Association, a significant honor. In the planning for his introduction as the president of the American Heart Association before several thousand cardiologists, it was felt that the world should see one of Dr. Harvey's teaching conferences. They had planned to demonstrate Dr. Harvey's new concept for physician education at home using TV. Guess what! They decided to use the conference that did not have the heart sounds that Dr. Harvey had become so famous for demonstrating. Instead of heart sounds, the engineers dubbed in sounds of toilet flushing, railroad crossing noises, racing car motors, thunder, wind, and rain storms. It brought the roof down with laughter. I sheepishly hid in the back of the room in darkness. In typical Dr. Harvey fashion, he told me he thought it was great that I had made this mistake!

We gave a lot of thought about staying in practice in Washington DC with the physician who had allowed me to have a nighttime practice in his office. However, the Vietnam War was accelerating, and I was still part of the Berry Plan. I had to make arrangements to enter the air force on active duty. I had been accepted into the air force's Berry Plan as an internal medicine physician. I, however, wanted to go in as a cardiologist. Approximately the same time in 1970, Dr. Charles Davidson called and asked if I would go back to Boston as the chief resident in internal medicine on the Harvard Medical Service. The BCH chief residents were MDs who had not only completed their internal medicine training but had also completed training in a subspecialty. This was a great honor, and I wanted to do it if possible.

To do this I would have to change my deferment for another year and, hopefully, change my deferment to cardiology. I did not realize protocol, and so one day I went to the head of the medical division for the US Air Force in Washington DC. I had made an appointment and walked in to present my plan regarding going back to Boston as chief resident. He thought that was a great opportunity and immediately, without hesitation and with a mere stroke of his pen, allowed me to take another year deferment and return to Boston. He said that following that year I would come into the air force as a cardiologist, so he had also changed my classification! This was another amazing bit of grace in my life.

CHAPTER 8

Chief Resident Year: Back to Boston

When we returned to Boston, we found a great apartment to live in Framingham, Massachusetts. I started as the chief resident of the Harvard II-IV Medical Service at BCH in July 1971. That was an incredible year and opened up many opportunities in the future. That job was a teaching job, and I had the title of instructor of medicine at Harvard Medical School. It was hard to believe that the boy who wasn't supposed to make it to college much less through medical school was now on the Harvard faculty! There were many incredible things that happened during that year. One of the most memorable events was recorded by Dr. Sheldon Rubenfeld. He became a very respected endocrinologist in Houston, and I believe has cared for both President and Barbara Bush. He wrote the introduction to the book *Medicine after the Holocaust: From the Master Race to the Human Genome and Beyond*. This book was published in conjunction with the Holocaust Museum in Houston and contains a series of lectures given on the topic. Shelly founded the Center for Medicine after the Holocaust (http:medicineaftertheholocaust.org), and I believe he has taught medical ethics at Rice University, Baylor College of Medicine, and the University of Texas Health Science at Houston.

Shelley was one of the outstanding medical students at Georgetown University Medical School. He had rotated through cardiology, and I had been involved with some of his teaching. I was so convinced the training at the BCH was the best in the world that I must have influenced him to do his internship there. In the introduction to this book, Shelley tells a story about an incident that occurred during his internship while I was chief resident. It is placed here to demonstrate an independent description of me during my year as chief resident at BCH in 1971.

Shelly describes the incident of a one-hundred-year-old women who was admitted to our service. The patient had been demented for many years and had been completely confined to bed for several years. She had no living relatives and no visiting friends. She was in great pain from gangrene of the leg and had advanced signs of dehydration.

Several interns, including Shelly, wished to put her out of her misery with an injection of potassium. I found out about their plans and, as chief resident, arranged for a meeting of all involved.

These young physicians were all from eastern schools and, typical of that era, had long hair with secular progressive ideas. In his writing, Shelly refers to me as a short-haired conservative leader from an "alien nation," Texas. "Worse," I was described as religious. I had never spoken to them about my religious beliefs and find it curious that during those restless years of the Vietnam War, Shelly somehow knew I was "religious" and had a strong belief in God.

I told them that I knew what they were planning and that they would not put this patient "out of her misery." They were told to never consider such a thing again. They must provide her with pain relief, IV fluids, oxygen, and antibiotics. My last words were, "Doctors do not kill patients. That's not what we do!"

This apparently had a great effect on Shelly. He has spent many years challenging medical personnel to personally confront the medical ethics of the Holocaust and apply that knowledge to contemporary practice and research. The whole collection, published by Palgrave Macmillan in 2010, is well worth reading. Many years later, Shelly asked me if I remembered this incident. He thanked me for teaching him what he felt was the most important lesson of his medical career.

In my chief medical residency year, I felt I was invincible and new everything necessary to be a great doctor. Years later, I realized it was only part of a stage in life that many of us pass through to gain wisdom. However, at the time it was real in my mind.

So the story goes that the medical interns would be taking their board exams and needed to be off for sleep the night before the exam. These Harvard interns really did not need to study, they just needed sleep. I volunteered to cover the intern duty on two floors by myself. I felt I could handle anything and was tough enough to do the job. It was a very difficult night, but I survived. Fortunately, no patients suffered from my foolish ego.

In the middle of the night, I got a call from the emergency room for a "DL" patient, as they were called in those days. At the BCH, a critically ill patient was placed on the "danger list," i.e., the "DL." All DL patients had to be accompanied during transfer from the emergency room by a ward physician. That meant I had to leave my two floors and go to the emergency room to bring this lady back to the floor. She was in paroxysmal supraventricular tachycardia. On arrival to the emergency room, I found the lady to have a stable blood pressure, but her heart rate was 220 beats per minute. All the usual techniques had not worked to convert her to normal rhythm. I needed to get her back to the floor, where I could convert her electrically if the medications have not worked by that time.

In the emergency room at the BCH, there were frequently nights with no transport people. This was one of those nights. I decided to bring the patient there myself. Nothing was impossible for this chief resident—or so I thought at the time. To get to the medical building, I had to roll the patient on her stretcher down a really steep ramp to reach the basement tunnels. Like interns, chief residents have their own uniform. We were the "upper class," so to speak, and could wear a shirt, tie, and dress slacks. The short white jacket also indicated our importance. Back in that time it was common also to dress in wingtip shoes. The shoes were heavy, with multiple superficial small circular holes punched out in the superficial leather layer in their typical pattern. They also had slick leather soles with steel-cleated heels. I was wearing this type of shoe on my trip back to the medical floor.

Needless to say, as I started down the ramp pushing the stretcher, my feet began to slip. It was obvious that I was losing control of the stretcher. The hill was steep, and we began to pick up speed. It was in the middle of the night; no help was available to rescue us.

So the patient and I began to careen down the steep ramp into the bowels of Boston City Hospital. This time of night there were no elevator operators to the basement floor where the tunnel to the medical building was located.

I had a vision of skating down the ramp with sparks flying off my cleated heels. I leaned down and told my patient that our stretcher was out of control but not to worry. I told her there was a sharp turn at the bottom of the hill and there would be a collision. She was strapped on the stretcher and there would not be any injury. I reassured her that she would be okay since she was going feet first, horizontal on the stretcher, securely strapped in.

Sure enough, we crashed into the wall and momentarily we both levitated. At that point the lady sat up and proclaimed, "It's gone!" Yes, the sudden jolt had cardioverted her back to normal rhythm. The following morning at the "morning report," I told the chief of service and my fellow residents that I had devised a new method for cardioversion. This was particularly cogent since I had already completed my cardiology training and, therefore, my opinion to the residents carried more weight with the residents than usual. The story was brought back to my attention by one of the interns who was sleeping that night before her board exams. I saw her at the fortieth reunion, and we shared "war stories."

There were many wonderful events during my year as chief resident. Trey was going to school in Newton, Massachusetts. It was a Montessori school. One of the students in that school was Vadu Bose, the son of Armor Bose. Pam became very good friends with Prima Bose, Vadu's mother. I remember having dinner in their apartment before the Bose speakers became so famous. I remember him telling us how he developed the speakers. Years later we returned to Boston, and the Boses took us to their new home on top of a large hill in western Boston.

Because of my two years of cardiology training, I had been made the director of the brand-new ICU on the Harvard Medical Unit at BCH. I remember the secretary of the service bringing me my letter from the US Air Force, which was believed to include my orders for going on active duty. The Vietnam War was in full swing, and I truly expected that I would end up being stationed somewhere in Vietnam. I nervously opened the letter. I was ecstatic to see that I was going to Scott Air Force Base in Illinois. I had visions of a hospital in a cornfield rather than a Vietnamese rice paddy. Thank you, God. More amazing grace!

CHAPTER 9

The Air Force Years

I spent two years on active duty at Scott Air Force Base, Illinois, just east of St. Louis, Missouri. I refer to those two years as my "early retirement." There was not enough room on base for air force housing, so we were allowed to live in a small Illinois community O'Fallon, Illinois. It was rented, but it was our first house. It was a fantastic little house, with a downstairs partial basement and the first floor being half a level above ground level. We had a great time during those years. Pam became pregnant with our fourth child while living there.

We were able to go home for Christmas 1973. After our vacation, on the way back home, we were stuck in the Dallas Love Field airport because of bad weather in St. Louis, Missouri. We had left our little green Datsun in the parking lot at the airport in St. Louis, which was across the Mississippi River from Scott Air Force Base. While in the Dallas airport, Pam went into labor again in her sixth month of pregnancy. Since the flight was delayed and Pam was in labor, we took all the kids in a taxicab to the Baylor University Hospital. The physician said that Pam had probably been in labor but it had stopped, so she could make the trip back to St. Louis. We returned to the airport to find people still waiting for our flight! We made the flight back to St. Louis and landed in one of the worst snowstorms and ice storms of that year. We got our bags, and I left Pam, Trey, Jarrod, and Hade waiting for me to go get our little green Datsun out of the parking lot.

On arrival to the parking lot by airport bus, I found a huge amount of snow with many snowdrifts. I could not find our little car and searched diligently in the freezing weather. I kept thinking I know I parked it right here, but there was a huge snowdrift. I wondered if it could be buried under the snow drift. I took my hands and scratched away the snow until I found my little green car completely buried in a snow and ice pack that was probably six-feet deep. There was nothing I could do. I returned to the airport and found my pregnant wife and three sons standing on the curb waiting for me with all the bags. I got out of the bus and relayed the story. I called our OB physician (Jack Kline) at Scott Air Force Base. He told us that all the bridges crossing the Mississippi were iced over and not passable. He said we should spend the night at a hotel at the airport, and he would try to come for us the following day. The following day was New Year's Day 1974.

We found a motel and all climbed in the room. The obstetrician had recommended alcohol as the means of preventing Pam from going back into labor. You can imagine the surprise of the bellhop who helped us all into our room on New Year's Eve when I said, "Find me a bottle of vodka and some orange juice. I need to keep my wife drunk so she will not go into labor." In those days, it was not appreciated that alcohol would be detrimental to the baby. The following morning, Jack Klein—who was our neighbor in O'Fallon, Illinois, and a good friend—and Pam's obstetrician drove across the ice-covered bridges to retrieve us from our imprisonment at the St. Louis airport. It was at least a week before I could retrieve the little Datsun from the airport.

Jack's recommendation was to try and get Pam to complete the nine months of pregnancy rather than have an early delivery as she had done in 1969 with Hade. Pam was in and out of the hospital with premature labor for the next month. Each time, the labor was stopped by using pure ethanol with orange juice. It was a crazy few months, but Christopher King Cashion arrived by cesarean section at approximately eight o'clock in the morning on February 20, 1974.

While in the air force, I moonlighted at St. Louis County Hospital's emergency room. I experienced some amusing encounters with patients there. One brief example is the mother who arrived with her very obese teenage daughter, and I realized that her daughter's abdominal pains were labor pains. When I told the lady she was about to become a grandmother, she fainted. I then had two patients to care for—one on the floor unconscious and the other in labor!

There were many other episodes I had during my two-year commitment to the active duty US Air Force at Scott Air Force Base. My plan was to go into private practice after my commitment was completed. If I had stayed in the air force I would have been offered a promotion to Lieutenant Colonel, but I decided private practice was where I wanted to be. When I finally separated from the air force a year later, I had a total for thirteen years' service, since they counted my medical school time and all my training.

My two years at Scott Air Force Base occurred during the Vietnam War. I felt blessed that I did not have to leave the continental United States for my service during that time. The only active connection I had with the war process was my dealing with the return of the POWs. It was very interesting and sad hearing the stories of men who had been imprisoned for up to seven or eight years. Their treatment had been horrible until the North Vietnamese realized the war was coming to an end and began to ease up on their harsh treatment. The saddest story I recall was from a man who had been reported as dead. His wife had remarried after many years of thinking he was dead. These men were all "locked up" for debriefing. A few of us physicians felt we needed to stage a jailbreak and took some of them to the officers' club. These "prisoners" greatly appreciate our efforts. We all got into trouble but escaped a court-martial. Later we all received a commendation from President Nixon for our work in "Operation Homecoming."

CHAPTER 10

The Waco Years

Wayne Falcone had been a cardiology fellow with me at Georgetown University. He did not have the extra year deferment so went into the air force earlier than I did. He ended up going into practice in Waco, Texas, following his two years in the air force. On our vacations, I would come to Waco to cover for Charlie Shoultz and Wayne so they could go hunting. It turns out that relationship resulted in our deciding to come to Waco for my first job in the private practice of medicine with Charlie and Wayne. It was a great experience with two excellent physicians and a fantastic job offer.

We were able to "buy" our first home. (Of course, the house was owned by the mortgage company and the builder who loaned me the down payment!) It was our "lifetime" house, and we had no plans to ever leave Waco.

In approximately June 1975, we were getting ready to leave on a vacation. Everyone was packed and in the car. I had returned to lock up the house when I heard the phone ring. That phone call changed my life in another direction. Rowdy (Pam's brother) was on the phone and related that Boppie was in the hospital after suffering a heart attack. We changed our plans; rather than going on our two-week vacation, we headed to Austin, Texas. Boppie was very sick and needed to be evaluated for possible coronary bypass surgery. In those days there were no coronary interventions available. I had sent many patients to Houston for complicated heart surgery and knew a heart surgeon, Dr. Jimmy Howell, by reputation but had never met him. I felt like I knew him, since I had had many phone calls with him regarding my patients. I felt that Boppie would likely need heart surgery, and I wanted Jimmy to do the surgery. Dr. Howell used a group of cardiologists that was headed by Dr. Don Chapman and Dr. Liston Beasley. I made arrangements for Boppie's transfer to the Methodist Hospital of Houston.

Boppie and I made the trip in an ambulance from Breckinridge Hospital in Austin to the Methodist Hospital emergency room in Houston in June 1975. I remember arriving in the emergency room of Methodist Hospital and meeting Dr. Liston Beasley, who was there to take care of Boppie. Boppie was admitted to the ICU and underwent cardiac catheterization by Dr. Beasley the next day. He, in fact, did need coronary bypass surgery. I went with Boppie to the operating room and was there as Dr. Howell did the coronary bypass surgery. Postoperatively, I remained with Boppie. Pam and the kids joined us in Houston and stayed with some friends. Since I had made arrangements to be off for approximately two weeks, I spent that entire time with Boppie. In those days, it was frequent that people stayed in the hospital ten the fourteen days following coronary bypass surgery. During that time interval, Drs. Chapman and Beasley invited me to make rounds with them on their patients at Methodist Hospital.

One day while having lunch with Dr Beasley, he asked me if I knew anyone who could join them in practice. One of their partners had recently had a heart attack and had dropped out of practice, and they definitely need someone urgently. I made the comment that I couldn't think of anybody just offhand. That night when I relayed the story to Pam she said, "You have just been offered a job." I told her I didn't think that was the case but I would check the next day. When I was next with Dr. Beasley, I asked him if I could apply for the position. He laughed and said that since I was one of their referring physicians they would have to be evasive, since they did not want to anger Charlie or Wayne. Clearly they wanted me to join their group. He had been afraid that I would not respond to his initial inquiry. Four months later, I started my job with Dr. Beasley and Dr. Chapman. They were known then as "The Chapman Group" when I started. In later years, we incorporated and it was changed to Houston Cardiovascular Associates.

Again more of God's grace! I had always been interested in private practice and academic medicine, and God delivered this opportunity without even a prayer to provide it for me. He knew what I wanted and needed—*what a miracle*! I worked at the Methodist Hospital for the next nineteen years. I started in October 1975 at the age of thirty-four. Many things happened during that time, by the grace of God. I progressed up the ranks of Baylor College of Medicine from a clinical assistant professor of medicine to a full clinical professor of medicine. I became president of the prestigious Methodist Hospital medical staff and was a full partner in the oldest cardiology group in Houston,

Texas. If one looks at my life as I am doing with this book, it is clear that God made incredible things happen. I, however, did not realize His influence until the next phase of my life in College Station, Texas—but first the Houston years.

CHAPTER 11

The Houston Years

To make the move to Houston, a lot of things had to happen. It was very difficult to tell Charlie and Wayne about my offer and my desire to go to Houston to practice with Drs. Chapman, Beasley, Winters, and Spencer. I finally was able to accomplish telling them. They were very kind in accepting the decision, and we have remained friends through the years. We had to sell our "lifetime" house and find a new house in Houston. That could not be accomplished in the time remaining before I had to start work in Houston. Our family was good friends with the Mendel family in Houston. They owned a place on Lake Inks, which was very close to our extended family's place. Mrs. Mendel invited me to live in their garage apartment. The last person who had lived in that garage apartment was her son Christopher, who had died on Lake Inks in a skiing accident several years before. She said that the garage apartment had been totally untouched since his death and my coming would be a great opportunity for her to get in there and clean things up. She did exactly that, and the little garage apartment became my home for the next three or four months until I could find a home for my family move from Waco.

I began looking for homes at every opportunity. Pam and the kids would come to Houston as often as possible to help me look for a new home. After many prayers, we found a house on Mossycup. Bommie said I should put a Mother Seton metal that had been blessed in the front yard of the house we wanted. Bommie had become the international president of the Ladies of Charity and become very close to Mother Seton for intercessory prayers.

One night I drove out to the home on Mossycup and put the metal in the front yard. The people who owned the house were still in the house and had the lights on. They did not notice my car stopping or my walking up and putting something in the front yard. I placed the metal in the space between the curb and the grass. As a result, we were able to somehow pull off a deal with financing a house, continuing to pay for the house in Waco, and arranging for the move to Houston. All of this was certainly another miracle—*another miracle by the grace of God.*

It took a long time to sell our house in Waco. We virtually gave it away at a loss so that we would not have two house payments. Though this was disappointing, it was balanced by the fact that things were going very well in the practice of cardiology at Houston Cardiovascular Associates. It was all I had hoped for. I became well known for my gifts as a physician, which God had given me. There were many miracles that I witnessed during my years at Houston. I will relate a few that I remember in great detail; there were many others.

Dr. Bill Spencer and I became known for implanting dual chamber pacemakers. At the time there were not many cardiologists implanting pacemakers, and most places had the vascular surgeon implant the pacemaker generator with the cardiologist putting in the single right ventricular lead. The dual chamber pacemaker changed things, with the atrial lead requiring a lot of time and manipulation. Most surgeons in those days were so busy doing coronary bypass operations, they did not want to mess with these new pacemakers. Dr. Howell helped Dr. Spencer and I become proficient at the surgical placement of the pacemaker generator and we developed techniques for placing the atrial lead, which was the new part of the device. In those days, the atrial lead was a passive fixation lead with tiny little tines at the end that had to be guided into a location that was stable with good electrical measurements. Because of our reputation, we were sent complicated cases.

One patient I received was in need of adding an atrial lead to her single chamber pacer, making it a dual chamber pacemaker. She had had bilateral mastectomies, which made the implementation of the larger generator difficult. It turned out that the implantation of a generator was the easiest part. The atrial lead, which was necessary for her condition, was impossible to place. I tried every trick in the book and was unable to place the pacemaker lead in a stable position. After over an hour of trying to place the atrial pacemaker lead, I walked over to the corner of the operating room and sat on the metal stool there and began to pray. My prayer was simply for Jesus to help me, since I was unable to help this lady and complete the operation. While I was sitting on the stool saying my prayer, one of the nurses said, "Dr. Cashion, the atrial lead is now working." She asked what I had done. I said to her, "You saw me. I was sitting in the corner of the operating room totally away from the patient. Now you tell me that the lead is working properly." They again asked how I did it. I told all in the operating room that I was praying that Jesus would help us. The patient was only lightly sedated, as we did that type of pacemakers operation under local anesthesia. The patient heard this conversation and asked what was going on. I walked over to her and said the lead seems to be working now. We checked it out diligently, and the thresholds were perfect. The lead position on fluoroscopy was also perfect. The lady kept asking, "What's going on?" I told her that I had been unable to place the atrial lead, but my prayers had been answered. I told her that Jesus had placed the lead perfectly in her atrium. I followed this lady's care for several years. Each time she arrived, she would ask, "How do you think the lead Jesus put in is working?" Every time we checked the lead, all the measurements were perfect, as you might expect. This was clearly a miracle. Thank you, Jesus!

Another miracle occurred during one of the many cardiac catheterizations I did while at the Methodist Hospital. We used to do most of them by the Sones technique, which involved doing a cutdown on the brachial artery of the arm. This particular patient had had four prior cut-downs on his right brachial artery. I was doing the fifth cut-down. I probably should have chosen to do the procedure from the left arm, but it was believed at that time that the left arm could be very difficult. The diagnostic angiogram went well, but as I was picked up the artery to begin making the repair, it disintegrated. Both ends of the artery retracted, one up the arm and one down the arm with severe arterial bleeding. I was able to retrieve both ends of the artery and stop the bleeding with rubber tipped "bulldog" clamps. I called the patient's doctor, who was one of the famous heart surgeons at the Methodist Hospital, to ask him to come and help repair the artery. The surgeon said he was in the operating room doing a complicated heart surgery and all the resident helpers were also busy. He told me to go ahead and fix it myself. I stated that I had watched many of these types of repairs but had never done one! He felt comfortable that I could repair the artery even though I had never done such a thing. In those days, malpractice issues and hospital privileges were less of an issue. The normal repair of the brachial cutdown was simple closure of a small hole in the front side of the artery. I had done that successfully many times. This would be reconnecting two very frayed artery segments. I proceeded with many prayers and repaired the artery. Following the procedure, the patient had a good right radial pulse and no bleeding. That evening on rounds, the surgeon and I saw the patient. The patient was doing very well with no problems from my arterial repair. The surgeon made a comment that he knew I could do it. I admitted to him that I didn't do it—God did the repair. God's hands had clearly directed the repair, since the surgeon could not be there. He just laughed and went on his way. I knew God had allowed me to repair that artery perfectly.

A third miracle was related to a patient who was dying in the operating room because of the complicated heart surgery. The surgical team could not get the patient off the heart-lung machine and called me to see if I could help. When I arrived to the operating room, it was clearly a desperate situation. The patient was not doing well. I worked my way to the head of the operating table and peered over the drapes into the open chest.

The Road From Troas

The heart was very dilated and poorly contracting. The patient could not generate enough blood pressure to sustain life and was still being maintained on the heart-lung machine. I reviewed everything that had been done. They had done everything that was possible, and I had little to add. The patient's face and head were right below me. He had a breathing tube in place and was on a breathing machine. I put my hands on his head and said a prayer for God to spare this man's life. Within a short period of time, the heartbeat was stronger. The patient subsequently came off the heart-lung machine and left the hospital.

Many people would say all these miracles were just luck, coincidence, or time for the medications to work. In my mind, however, it was my prayer and faith that God could certainly change the tide of events and allowed these people to recover.

A fourth miracle was an ongoing series of events with a dear patient of mine named Marshall. This story will jump ahead in my life and may confuse you regarding timing of events. I will be mentioning things that you won't understand until later. His story is so incredible that I had to mention it along with the other miracles I have witnessed. His miracle was a series of events that covered over twenty years. Marshall and I first met when he was brought to Methodist Hospital during his first heart attack at age forty. He had a cardiac arrest on the way to the hospital and was being maintained with CPR. It was a resuscitative effort that was complicated by our inability to place a breathing tube because of a peculiar neck curvature and his large size. Again with prayers, he gradually improved. He suddenly woke up while still on the stretcher in the emergency room. Since he did not have a breathing tube in place, he could speak. He looked at me and said, "Doctor, why are you concerned? I'm coming to your funeral." That started a long and wonderful relationship with Marshall.

His heart was so damaged by his first heart attack that he ended up needing a cardiac transplant. He was one of the few people in the world that ended up with a double heart transplant. The donor heart had to be large enough to supply this large body. The first heart was from a small lady. His situation was so severe the team decided to do a heterotopic heart transplant, where they put the new heart in his right chest and left his old heart pumping in the left chest. Within a couple of months, however, his old heart on the left side of the chest stopped working completely and he went back into heart failure. After much discussion, a second heart transplant was accomplished with a new transplant on the left side, replacing the heart he was born with. At that point Marshall had two transplanted hearts: the first transplant in the right chest and the second transplant in the left, in the normal position. When he woke up from the second operation I was with him. Marshall had a great sense of humor, and his first question, "Was that another lady donor?" When I answered yes and explained that the second donor had also been a young lady killed in a car accident, he said, "I thought so. I have this intense desire to shop!"

I told Marshall following those two transplants that I did not deal with transplant patients and he would need to be followed by the transplant group. He was disappointed but went on his way.

Several months later, Marshall returned to my office unexpectedly and stated that he was having a rejection of the first transplanted heart, the one in his right chest. He was getting into trouble. I stated that I'm sure everything was being done that could be done. His answer was an emphatic no! He said, "No one is praying with me! I will get better if you pray with me that I will get better." That morning in my office, we prayed that Marshall would get better. His transplant rejection completely resolved. He had two other episodes of similar transplant rejection. Both of these episodes resulted in him coming back to me so that we could pray together that he would get better. Each time he got better! Of course, the transplant people took credit for knocking out the rejection process. Marshall and I, however, felt our prayers had made the difference. We talked about this often and actually did several radio shows regarding his miraculous recovery from the three heart transplant rejections. Marshall's complicated health issues went on for a number of years. When I moved to College Station, he continued to come there for me to follow him and pray with him. We always prayed together when we met; this was at Marshall's insistence. I learned a lot from Marshall's faith.

One day he told me he didn't feel well. Prior to that day, his EKG was amazing in that it would show two normal EKGs superimposed on each other. On that day, his EKG showed only one normal-appearing EKG. That meant one of the transplanted hearts was not working—flat line! He was sent back to the transplant team. There was a lot of discussion of what to do. When evidence of peripheral blood clots appeared from his nonfunctioning transplanted heart, the decision was made to remove the dead heart. It was the first transplanted heart. The team was hopeful that Marshall would do well with only one heart, the second transplanted heart, in the normal position in his left chest. Pam, our friend Cindy, and I went to Methodist Hospital in Houston to be with Marshall and his wife. The operation was successful, and the first transplanted heart was removed.

When I later moved to Salado, I lost track of Marshall for a few years. One day he called to ask if I would be with him on *The Oprah Winfrey Show*. Oprah's team had somehow heard of Marshall's story and was thinking of doing a show with him. I of course agreed, but it never happened. Marshall's course became complicated with renal failure and pneumonia. Marshall survived until a couple of years ago, over twenty years following his first transplant! I know Marshall believed and I certainly believe that his survival for that duration was clearly miraculous.

At Methodist Hospital, I had the opportunity to take care of many famous people. I will mention a few of their names but will not go into each of their very interesting histories. I took care of Charlie Wilson of *Charlie Wilson's War*. He was the US Representative from Lufkin, Texas, who was involved with the overthrow of Russia in Afghanistan. His story has been published, and I was mentioned in his book regarding his heart problem. I was able to take care of Elizabeth Taylor on one occasion. For those of you who may not know, she was a very famous movie star known for her beauty and blue-green eyes. Because of Don Chapman's reputation, I was able to care for many people when he was unavailable. These patients included Mr. Ben Taub, whom the public hospital in Houston is named after; Dr. Michael DeBakey, who is really responsible for the development of the Texas Medical Center; and one of the finance ministers of Saudi Arabia. All these episodes were amazingly interesting, but I will not go into any of the details.

At Methodist Hospital, I became close friends with a famous surgeon, Dr. Jimmy Howell. He had a phenomenal success with surgery. Jimmy was the surgeon whom we had sent all of our surgical patients to when I was in practice in Waco. He was also the surgeon who had done Boppie's surgery and led to my move to Houston. Jimmy and I had many wonderful experiences and became very close friends. I became the physician for his lovely wife, Roberta. After I had been in Houston for a few years, Jimmy and Roberta asked me to be executor of their six children's estate. That was during the time Jimmy was acquiring a substantial amount of acreage in Liberty County. My four boys and Jimmy's youngest two boys became friends.

While in Houston, I also became an acquaintance of Dr. Denton Cooley. In my early years in Houston, I took care of a lawyer who was a senior member of one of the large lawyer groups in Houston. He and Denton Cooley had been basketball players at the University of Texas and had been members of the famous group at the University of Texas known as the "Cowboys." This group can be seen at all the University of Texas games when they shoot the cannon off after a football score. They all wear leather chaps and help with Bevo, the UT mascot. Back in the old days, the initiation to the Cowboys involved branding a UT on the newly initiated person's chest. When I examined this lawyer for the first time, I noticed a UT scar on his chest. He laughed and said that was part of the initiation. He said that he and Denton Cooley had been branded on the same night. He knew that I was a part of the Methodist Hospital group but made it very clear that if he ever needed heart surgery he wanted Dr. Cooley to do the surgery at St. Luke's. That lawyer arranged for me to play golf with Denton Cooley for several years to be sure that we were friends and I would feel comfortable in calling him if the lawyer needed heart surgery. Getting to know Dr. Cooley was a great experience. The senior partner of my group, Dr. Don Chapman, was a close friend of his. Many of our patients had Dr. Cooley for their surgeon, and I witnessed several operations at St. Luke's hospital performed by Dr. Cooley. That was an amazing experience. I became convinced that at that time, the two best surgeons in the world were Dr. Denton Cooley and Dr. Jimmy Howell.

When I was vice president of the medical staff at the Methodist Hospital, I was requested to attend a medical meeting in Athens, Greece, with Dr. Michael DeBakey. That was an amazing experience also. Dr. DeBakey flew separately from the rest of us. When we arrived in Athens, Dr. DeBakey was not there. We found out that he had been stuck in Germany because of a Lufthansa strike. We were supposed to have a news conference on our arrival, but he wasn't there. He arrived sometime later that night, while we were all asleep. We were rousted out of our beds to go to the conference. The next morning, I drug myself out of bed to get ready to go to Delphi for talks that we were all going to give. When I staggered into the hotel restaurant for breakfast, Dr. DeBakey was already there looking very alert. At the time he was in his early eighties. It was approximately 1990. He looked at me and asked what was the matter. I told him I had been a little tired with the journey and being up for our press conference. He made a casual comment of "Get with it, Cashion. We have a lot of work to do today." We drove to Delphi, where we gave our presentations. We were having lunch at a restaurant when a helicopter arrived for Dr. DeBakey. He left the lunch and flew off to some island with one of his wealthy Greek patients.

On the way home I had an amazing experience, which was potentially life-threatening. We were taking off from the airport in Amsterdam. We had just become airborne and were probably a couple of thousand feet off the ground when suddenly there was a loud explosion-type sound. All the lights in the airplane went off, and it seemed like the motors died. A few seconds later, the pilot came on the PA system as the motor started back up and the lights came on. He said, "We have just been struck by lightning." He made a very casual comment that everything seems to be fine and were headed home across Atlantic. We made the trip safely with the help of God, but it was an incredible experience to be in an airplane that was struck by lightning and lost power for a brief moment. The way things are today, I'll bet the airplane would've turned around and landed to allow for a more sophisticated evaluation. That episode made me feel I had something left in my life that could be important to our Lord.

In those days, we frequently went sailing on Lake Conroe. We had a condominium and a ski boat at Walden on Lake Conroe. We spent many weekends there. Pam and I love sailing, and we frequently bought friends along in a rented thirty-two-foot sailboat. One beautiful day, we started off on our rented sailboat journey. The young captain and I had arranged for me to do the sailing. It started off as a beautiful night. After about sixty minutes, a really bad thunderstorm blew up and all the passengers were ordered below. The young captain and I, as well as everyone on board, decided to continue the trip (big mistake!). The storm was much more severe than we thought. The waves became high, the wind became intense, and the lightning display was absolutely incredible. As the captain and I worked to gain control of the boat and sail us back to safety, I had one of those funny peaceful feelings, despite the danger we were experiencing. A voice in my soul said, "You are sailing into some tough times in your life. If you have faith in Me, I will lead you out of the storm." As we finally came into sight of our landing at Walden, the clouds suddenly cleared and it became a beautiful clear night with bright, shining stars. I interpreted this feeling exactly as it happened: storm, then beautiful peace. I had sailed into a storm, and God would deliver me.

I started to have a repetitive dream. I remember standing by a white fence. There were three small white horses behind the fence in a green field. I was talking with a nun of the Daughters of Charity order. She was in her full nun regalia with her tall winglike hat. Those readers old enough to remember the TV series called *The Flying Nun* will know how she was dressed.

I would wake up from this dream feeling nothing but happiness and joy. I remember talking to the nun in the dream and that I was very happy, but I had no idea of what we were talking about. The dream was so frequent that I discussed it with Pam. I had no idea where I was in the dream and began to search for that place.

I started to think I was having a midlife crisis. One day while sitting in our Inks Lake home living room, I was looking through a magazine and found a picture of little horses and a green field. It was similar but not identical to my dream. It turned out that the article was about a monastery just west of Navasota, Texas, where the sisters were raising miniature horses.

Pam and I made a journey one Sunday to see that monastery and spend an afternoon wandering around and visiting with the nuns. When we left, Pam asked me if it did anything for me. I said no. However, from that day forward I never had the dream again. I began having another recurrent dream. In this new dream I would find where I was to go while sitting at my desk in the Houston Cardiovascular Associates office. As I woke up, I could again feel the happiness of this possibility.

I really began feeling I was having a midlife crisis. I was around fifty-three years of age. I began looking through my mail very carefully and listening to every phone conversation carefully, wondering if and when I would find where I was supposed to go. Our fourth son, Christopher, was at the University of Arkansas as a freshman. The Christopher story is another miracle, but that's about Chris and Cindy, his tutor. I am hopeful that Christopher and Cindy will write the story of his miracle someday. All of you that know our family know the Christopher story very well. Christopher had significant dyslexia and wanted to transfer to Texas A&M University from Arkansas. His girlfriend, Joy, had started her freshman year there. Due to one of the many Christopher blessings, he was able to transfer to Texas A&M after his first semester as a freshman at the University of

Arkansas by making a 4.0 grade point average. Through his faith and courage with many prayers and help from his parents, tutor, and multiple friends, he ended up graduating from dental school with honors and a citation on his clinical excellence in dental surgery. Enough said regarding that miracle. I'll briefly discuss it later.

Since Christopher was coming to the University of Texas A&M, I felt it would be important for him to have a physician friend in the community. Dr. Phil Alexander had been a good referring physician to my Houston practice, and I had gotten to know him very well. I arranged for a dinner one evening with Christopher and Dr. Alexander. During that dinner, Phil asked me if I would consider starting a heart program at his hospital in College Station, which was called the Brazos Valley Medical Center in those days. I said that was nonsense since I was president of the medical staff at Methodist Hospital, a clinical professor of medicine at Baylor College of Medicine, and a full partner of one of the oldest cardiology practice in Texas. For those of you who know Phil, you know he can be persistent.

Because of Phil's persistence, some people at the Brazos Valley Medical Center began to think I might come to start a heart program there. Things got out of hand. I felt I needed to meet with them person-to-person to tell them that, even though it was an interesting offer and a great compliment, there was no way that I could do it. It was such a crazy idea that I didn't bother to tell my partners about it that stormy spring afternoon when I left to go meet these people and tell them I was not coming.

As I started driving to College Station, the weather became intense, with threats of severe thunderstorms and even tornadoes. That was the only afternoon I could take off and the people were expecting me to come, so I felt I had to make the trip. I could not cancel a whole afternoon of office patients and not use the time for something important. As I was driving, I kept thinking, *"Dear God, if I'm not supposed to do this, let me know"*. On coming through Navasota, I heard a radio report that there may be a tornado in the area. I kept driving toward College Station. As I turned off on Rock Prairie Road, the sky was intensely black and I actually felt concern for my safety. I picked up my mobile phone to call Phil and the group of people waiting for me at the hospital to tell them I was heading home and not coming. At that very moment, I was crossing the bridge on Rock Prairie Road when the sunlight broke through of clouds and the entire sky turned an incredibly beautiful red color—not orange or pink—a deep red. The Holy Spirit's color is red. I said to myself, *Alright, God, I'll go meet these people.* That most incredible sunset changed my mind. From that time on, I have paid close attention to beautiful sunsets and sunrises.

I walked into the administrative office of the hospital to meet the people wanting me to discuss starting a cardiology program. After brief introductions, I walked over to the window and told them to look at the sunset. I said, "The only reason I came to this meeting was because of that sunset. I was about to make a U-turn and head back home. I thought that the inclement weather was a sign that I should not come here. That sunset changed my mind. "If you think that's a little crazy, that's me. If you don't like that type of person, then you have the wrong person and we need not go any further." We obviously went further in that discussion. It led to my decision to leave all the things I had accomplished in Houston and start a new practice. I felt God had spoken to me. This time, I felt, I was following what God wanted me to do. The sunset was His sign. In fact, I began to feel God frequently speaking to me with sunsets, resulting in great happiness when I am doing His work.

On the drive home, I called Pam to tell her what had happened and that I felt we needed to strongly consider moving to College Station to start a heart program. Pam pointed out the obvious—we needed to sell our house and needed to buy a new house. There was no concern about selling our Mossycup house, since someone had recently walked up to our door and asked if they could buy it. The house was not for sale, and there was no sign suggesting its sale. No one knew we were considering a move. The man had just liked our house and offered to buy it. We made plans to look for a home in College Station and proceed with selling our Houston home.

One afternoon, Pam and I decided to go to College Station and look for a house. Cindy Crosswhite was Christopher's tutor, and we asked her to go along for the trip. I don't remember exactly how it happened, but we got lost driving through the country roads. As we were driving, we passed a wonderful house. I made a casual comment that if we were to move to this area, it would be nice to have a house like that and live in the country. We went down the road a little further and the dirt road came to a T. We turn left and drove alongside a white fence on the right side. The trees on the right suddenly cleared, and there was a large pasture of green grass, probably winter wheat, with three little white horses standing close to the white fence. I stopped the car. Pam had heard me talk about the dreams enough that she asked if this look familiar. I said it did, except there was no Daughter of Charity nun standing at the fence.

Shortly after that we went to a real estate agent to make a more serious look for a new home. We had never met the real estate agent, and she did not know anything of my prior vision or of us seeing the house. We made a comment that we were considering moving from Houston and it might be nice to live in the country after living in a big city for nineteen years. The real estate agent said that there was a house that was possibly coming on the market that might fit our needs. She pulled out a series of pictures. On viewing the pictures, we discovered it was the identical house that we had driven by on the afternoon when we saw the white horses behind the white fence. She said the people had not decided yet to sell the house but they were thinking seriously about it. We made arrangements to see the house. The minute I walked into the house, I knew that it was the house we would be living in. Pam was not so sure. We looked at many houses. The people finally decided to sell her home, and we were able to buy the house we had seen close to the three white horses. We had sold our Houston house to the man who had walked up and wanted to buy it. I truly felt God was telling us to make the move to College Station and leave all the professional achievements God had given us. We lived in that house in College Station for the next ten years.

CHAPTER 12

The College Station Years

The move to College Station changed my life again in a dramatic way. I had always been a spiritual and religious person, but the move to College Station introduced a trust in the Lord that I did not have before. There were so many experiences while we lived there that expanded my faith and brought me closer to my Lord and Savior Jesus Christ. I will try to remember as many of them as possible. I believe that the real change occurred one day when I was giving a lecture to the Christian Medical and Dental Society at Texas A&M University. They had asked me to discuss my training and how I had accomplished the things I had accomplished in my life.

I was giving a lecture in one of the auditoriums at the Texas A&M medical school when it happened. I was relating the story that I've described in this book up to this point. As I was giving the lecture, I had a peculiar sensation come over me. I believe the Holy Spirit informed me at that very moment that my entire life had been a gift from God. All the things that I thought I had accomplished with my hard work had been gifts from God. So here I was giving the "how great I am" lecture and suddenly realized all the things I'd accomplished were not from my hard work. My eyes were opened to the fact that what I had accomplished was truly impossible. The great success had all occurred because the Lord wanted it to happen and made it happen.

So here I was standing in front of these medical and dental students giving a lecture when I suddenly became tearful. I couldn't speak for a moment. At that point I looked up at these eager medical and dental hopefuls and told them I had just realized the incredible influence of God in my life and needed to change the lecture. I gave my first lecture that related all I had accomplished to a gift from God. You might say that was the first public expression of my understanding of how the little boy who was not supposed to make it through college had accomplish what he had accomplished. *It was truly the grace of God* that had allowed me to be successful.

As I had started my practice in College Station, I had many problems. Doctors are required to have extensive training in how to take care of patients but no training in the business of the practice of medicine. In starting a new solo practice of cardiology in College Station, I needed help. I asked my son Trey to come and assist me. Trey has an interesting story regarding how he ended up in office practice management and maybe someday he will write a book. Nevertheless, he moved from Dallas with his wife, Stephanie, and their young son, Treivor (William Richard Cashion IV) to help me. My second son, Jarrod, and his wife, Shannon, and their daughter, Lauren, had also moved to College Station to start a chiropractic practice.

Trey and I had mutual feelings regarding managed care. The influence of insurance companies and government on the daily practice of medicine was becoming onerous. We felt that the practice of medicine was no longer caring for patients as God intended. These institutions had gradually impinged on the patient–physician relationship, turning medical care into a commodity. Because of legal reasons and the "politically correct" mentality, God was left out of the practice of medicine. We were being directed by insurance companies as to what we could do and how we needed to do it. People were forced to make decisions they were not happy with to maintain insurance coverage. Trey and I felt that we needed to head in a different direction and began thinking of ways we could accomplish this. We began to talk about a healthcare system that was faith based not just in name but in the day-to-day, patient encounter to patient encounter process. We had seen the movie *Patch Adams* and began to think of a system that was based on faith rather than laughter, as *Patch Adams* had proposed. We prayed on it to consider that as a possibility and to consider starting an organization that would have the faith concept as its primary goal.

This organization would need a name. One day we decided to go home and pray as to what we would call this new health care concept. In those days, I used to open the Bible and read the first thing that caught my attention. I open the Bible to the Acts of the Apostles with Saint Luke talking about Saint Paul's trip to Troas (part of Saint Paul's second missionary journey). Saint Paul had arrived at Troas with intentions to go east to spread the gospel. He had a dream of a man in Macedonia, and in that dream the Holy Spirit directed Saint Paul to instead go west to Macedonia (Acts16:8–9). At a different time but also in Troas (Acts 20: 4–12), Saint Paul was giving a long sermon, and a young boy (Eutychus) fell asleep and fell from a high window. The boy was pronounced dead. When they went to see the boy, Saint Luke, who was a physician, did nothing since it was obvious the boy was dead. Saint Paul, on the other hand, through his faith and the grace of Jesus Christ raised the child from the dead. I have wondered if Saint Paul felt a little guilty about putting the boy to sleep with his sermon. Nevertheless, it was the spiritual act that saved the boy, not a medical act. I felt these passages from Acts of the Apostles had a direct relationship to what Trey and I were planning. They both occurred in Troas. Troas is also the place where Saint Luke joined Saint Paul on his second missionary trip. This is where the physician (Saint Luke) joined the first Christian missionary, Saint Paul the evangelist. We know this is the place where Saint Luke joined them, since he is the author of Acts of the Apostles and changes from writing in the third person to writing in the first person (Acts 16:–10). We felt this supported our feeling that medicine should head in the opposite direction from its current path. Remember Saint Paul and Saint Luke had changed direction in Troas. We felt we had to leave the Godless insurance concept that was driving a wedge between the physician–patient relationship. We felt that medicine needed to realign with our Christian faith and head a new direction. Spirituality had to be an important part of that new direction. It was also obvious that the new concept should be named Troas. So with some help we began filing the papers to start a not-for-profit ministry by the name of Troas. Trey made all the arrangements.

We felt we needed a logo for the concept. Christopher is an outstanding artist. Christopher drew a logo that represented our concept of this organization. The T of Troas was a large cross with a dove at the intersection of the crossbar, indicating our cross of salvation. The middle letters were individually spelled out as R O A, and the S was the symbol of the staff that Moses used when he raised up the bronzed snake in the desert (Numbers 21:4–9).

Charting, under His direction, a new course for medicine.

This is also the medical staff of Aesculapius and the old Greek symbol for medicine, which was the original caduceus. In the Old Testament, the Israelites had been unfaithful, and God sent the very poisonous snakes as a punishment. They came to Moses and had begged for assistance. God told them, through Moses, that if they look at the staff with the bronze snake and believed in Him, they would not die from the snakebite. They would recover. The same holds for looking at the crucifixion of Jesus as our Savior. Belief that Jesus saved us on the cross saves us. Both symbols remind us of the saving power of God.

We did a lot of studying regarding the medical caduceus commonly used in most places today, which has two snakes and wings. That symbol is commonly used to represent medical facilities and is really the symbol of the god Mercury. Mercury was a thief and one of the gods of the underworld. It seems strange that not many have questioned the double snake and winged caduceus commonly used these days to represent the medical profession. It sort of fits my feeling that medicine under the influence of insurance companies and government would pick the two snake, winged caduceus.

There were so many amazing things that happened in College Station. One Sunday I was on call and working at St. Joseph Hospital in Bryan, Texas. I was late getting to church. Pam said she and the boys would meet me there in the back. When I arrived late at church, I could not see Pam anywhere and wondered what had happened. She showed up smiling a few minutes later with the boys in tow and said she would tell me about it later.

What had happened was that she ran out of gas on the way to church. She had pulled into a gas station, luckily coasting right up to the gas pump. At the same time coming from the other direction, Peter Stulting ran out of gas headed the other direction. They had both coasted into the same gas station on the opposite side of the same pump. They were both driving the identical cars, which happened to be BMW 635i. Pam and Peter exchange comments regarding their cars and both running out of gas. Peter remarked that he was a radio show host. In the discussion, Peter had mentioned he was going to start a doctor's talk show. Pam had announced her husband was a physician. This led to a question that changed our lives. He asked if he might talk with me regarding starting the doctor's radio show. Of course, she answered yes. That coincidence started a ten year radio show called *Doctor's House Call*. I, of course, no longer believe in coincidences or serendipity. These type of events are God speaking to us; we just have to learn to listen. That was a Sunday. On Monday Peter and I met, and the first radio show was that Thursday. It became a weekly show. Initially we took call-ins but subsequently changed the format to a one-hour discussion with specific topics. Since I had gained strength in my spirituality, many of the shows were related to spirituality in medicine and my beliefs as a Christian physician. My past life was discussed on several occasions. The concept of Troas ministry was presented on several occasions.

I became known locally as a physician who was a Christian and openly expressed his beliefs in the office and operating room. I frequently prayed with my patients in the office and in the operating room before cardiac catheterizations or stent placement. I'm not sure I would've had the courage to do that at the Methodist Hospital in Houston. Another moment of amazing grace. What are the chances that Pam and Peter would both run out of gas at exactly the same time and end up in exactly the same type of car on opposite sides of the same gas pump?

Cindy Crosswhite helped with radio show. Her voice was so distinctive that she actually became a local celebrity with her voice being recognized in grocery stores and other places. It was the trio of Peter Stulting, Cindy, and I that made the radio show every Thursday. Ultimately the radio station built a radio studio in my office to make things easier. As a result of the radio show, we were invited to a weekly morning praise and worship service at the Hilton Hotel in College Station. Those meetings were excellent. On several occasions, we heard brief sermons from the minister at Central Baptist Church, Chris Osborne. Chris became a good friend and did several radio shows with us regarding issues of spirituality and medicine.

On another Sunday, I was on call and driving home after making morning rounds at St. Joseph Hospital. I happen to turn on the radio, which happened to be on an ongoing program that involved the Sunday service at Central Baptist Church. Chris Osborne was in the midst of his sermon. I did not hear the first part of it, but in the part that I heard, Chris was using me as an example of following the call of God. I took this as God telling me he was pleased with what I was doing. Again, what are the odds that I would turn on a radio driving in my car and have somebody speaking on the radio about my change in life, leaving Houston to follow what I felt was what God had asked of me. Whenever I feel God has spoken to me, I consider that a miracle—or is it just a blessing?

While all these things were happening, I was in the process of developing a cardiology program at the College Station Medical Center. The process involved starting with no cardiac catheterization facility and no heart surgery program. Over a few years, with God's grace, I was able to establish a program with two cardiac cath labs, open-heart surgery, and two additional partners. We had a full service cardiology office with treadmill testing, echocardiography, nuclear cardiology, and even enhanced external counter pulsation (EECP). EECP is a procedure used mostly to help patients with angina who cannot be helped with a coronary intervention.

An interesting aside, when I was chief resident at the BCH, I had been asked to be a consultant for the engineering program that developed ECP (External Counter Pulsation, as it was initially called). I actually was a part of the first demonstration of this type of equipment at the American Heart program in Anaheim, California, I believe in the fall of 1971. Our group in College Station was initially called Cashion Cardiology. Because of several conflicts, the name was changed to BCS Heart.

Pam and Cindy Crosswhite helped me run our office. I taught them both how to do EKGs and how to obtain a good medical history. Pam and Cindy were very good with patients and quickly became attached to all of them. They made the office a happy place, and patients loved to be there. When emergencies came up, I never worried about seeing an unhappy patient. They would either reschedule the patient if they could not wait or entertain them until I got there. With the developing cardiology program, cardiac catheterizations, and coronary interventions, unexpected emergency visits to the hospital frequently occurred. This made scheduling very difficult and somewhat stressful. Pam and Cindy, however, handled the situations fantastically.

One night one of our patients had a cardiac arrest and he passed away. The three of us went in to see his sad wife. We all wished at that moment that the College Station Medical Center had a chapel. As a result of that encounter, we began working diligently to build a hospital chapel in the College Station Medical Center. The chapel in that hospital was built because of that patient, our insistence, the hospital's commitment, and, of course, the help of the Good Lord.

The Road From Troas

One day I was asked to be the standby physician for the four presidents who were coming to the Bush Library for its dedication. Just prior to being asked to do that, the St. Joseph Hospital administration had asked Trey and I to attend a meeting of the Catholic Hospital Association in Austin, Texas, as their representative. We had accepted. I was therefore very disappointed when I was asked to be the physician on call for all of the presidents for the library opening. I had already accepted the Catholic hospital invitation and felt I could not do the presidential affair. The minute I told the people preparing for the president's library dedication that I could not do it, I had a feeling that it was the correct decision and something good would happen.

Trey and I were in Austin during all the presidential library festivities. We returned late that afternoon. Pam and Cindy, as well as the rest of our office staff, were doing blood pressure checks and cardiovascular screening at one of the shopping centers in Bryan Texas. I had just walked into the shopping center when my phone went off. It was Dr. Ben Orman calling. He was President Bush's personal physician in Houston, Texas, and wanted me to make a house call on President Bush. He said I would have to go to the presidential library to check on his condition. Ben said he would contact the Secret Service, and they would be waiting for me to take me to the president in his apartment above the library.

On arrival, the Secret Service took me to President Bush's bedroom. The president was sitting on the bedside with a robe over his shorts and socks. A quick examination demonstrated that he did not have a serious condition and his symptoms would not require any additional testing. Ben had told me that I should not take the president to our emergency room unless I felt he had a dangerous problem. If he needed hospitalization, he should go to Houston Methodist Hospital. Ben just wanted somebody with good clinical judgment to "lay hands" on the president to be sure there was nothing dangerous. After I completed the exam, I used my mobile phone to call Dr. Orman while I was standing at the president's bedside. I turned to President Bush to give him the good word that everything was okay and nothing needed to be done. President Bush opened his bedside table drawer and pulled out his billfold. He said, "What do I owe you?" I told him that being of service to him was one of the greatest honors in my life and that he did not owe me anything. He would not hear of it and kept persisting. I kept refusing. We finally reached a compromise, and he decided to take me on a personal tour of his apartment. As we walked through each room, he would pick things up off the desks and counters and stuff them in my pockets as souvenirs.

We were walking down the hall when he told me that he was going to take me into a place where no one gets to go. He opened the door and a very loud alarm went off, which was quite frightening since the alarm triggered the Secret Service agents to descend upon us rapidly. President Bush stood there with his robe open in only his undershorts and socks. He held his arms up and said, "Guys, it's okay. I just wanted to show Dr. Cashion Barbara's office." Barbara Bush was not there during that afternoon. She had gone to play golf, and I did not get to meet her.

I felt that the pain the president was experiencing was just muscle spasms. I called one of my chiropractor son's massage therapists and arranged for the president to have a massage that Friday evening. When I called the massage therapist and asked her to make a house call, she was a little reluctant. When I told her it was okay, it was President Bush, she said she would be there in ten minutes.

As I left the presidential library, I walked out to see one of those rare and beautiful sunsets that I have continued to feel is God trying to tell me something. I interpreted it that he was telling me I had made the right decision in going to the Catholic hospital meeting. He had arranged for me to see the president because of that. Shortly after that, a very unusual phenomena occurred. I was driving my car by the presidential library when a rainbow developed and actually entered the front window of the car. I was driving through a "sun shower." I have no idea what that rainbow meant. In my entire life, I have never seen rainbow other than a typical curve that one sees at a distance. The rainbow followed me for a brief time and then vanished. I'm only commenting on this happening since it was so unusual and special for unknown reasons.

It was about this time that Pam's mother, Bommie, became very ill with the stroke. Pam left College Station to be with her in Austin, Texas. I think I failed to mention that Boppie, Pam's father, had died a couple years before from cancer of the esophagus. One night while Pam was gone, I had a dream that Pam had cancer of the pancreas. She had been complaining of some back pain and abdominal pain. Because she was in Austin, we decided to wait until she got home for her evaluation. Her symptoms, however, seemed to be increasing. Following the dream, I called one of my friends in Austin and asked him if he could perform a CAT scan on Pam. I had made a comment to him that I was sure he had dealt with a lot of physicians and physician families but that this was probably the first time he had been asked to obtain a CAT scan because of a dream. He called me back later that day to tell me that, in fact, they had found far advanced cancer the pancreas on the scan. We subsequently went to MD Anderson hospital for consultation with the leaders in the field dealing with cancer of the pancreas. They told us that if we did nothing, she would live five or six months, probably three to four good months before she became limited. If we did surgery and chemotherapy, she might live up to a year but would spend most of the time in the hospital. Pam made the decision to do nothing, and we hoped for a few good months to do thing she wanted to do. I remembered the storm on Lake Conroe.

During that time, we saw many of our old friends and took a couple of wonderful trips. Although people came to comfort her, it was obvious that when they left they had been comforted. They had received more than they had given. Cindy Crosswhite and hospice care were both fantastic in helping with the problems that arise while dealing with a terminal cancer patient. I cut way back on my practice. I thank Mario Lammoglia and Marcel Lechin for helping me during the stressful time. They basically took over my practice and took care of the patients while I was busy with Pam.

The week before Pam left to be with God, she did an amazing thing. She was extremely weak and pretty much confined to the house. One of our patients was dying in a hospital extended care unit. He was having a great deal of trouble dealing with his situation. One day I was making rounds on him, and he had developed a totally different attitude. It was so remarkable that I asked him why he looked so relaxed and even happy. He said Pam had been by that day, and it had helped him with accepting his situation. I said, "That is impossible! Pam is at home and extremely weak." He said, "She was here today and helped me." The patient died the following day. The nurses in attendance said that he was very peaceful and had a "happy death."

The following day I thought I should go to the office to take care of some business. As I was driving down the road, I asked myself what I was doing and realized that I needed to be with Pam and not worry about the office. I returned home and found Cindy with Pam. Pam and Cindy had decided to go to Houston to shop. We all decided that would be fun and, despite Pam's weakened condition, we would go. Hospice had provided a wheelchair. We packed it up and went to Houston. We had an outstanding time. The three of us had a very happy and fun-filled day. Approximately two days later (on Dec 14, 1998), Pam died in our home in College Station.

How do you describe the end of a thirty-nine year relationship? It's impossible to relate that time and events in my life related to Pam's death. It is difficult to write about it seventeen years later! I remember sadness, loneliness, despair, and a great void in my life that had been filled every day of my life for almost forty years by Pam. I remember what Pam told me just prior to her death, and her concept has sustained me through the years.

One day she asked me how I would deal with her winning the most incredible trip anyone could ever take if it came with the only problem—I could not go with her. She described her vision of heaven and the wonderful things she would be encountering. She said it will be the greatest trip ever, followed by incredible joy and excitement and total peace. No pain, hunger, sadness, or any of the negative emotions humans have felt since the fall of man ... only *love*! She told me to think about what she would be doing and not on the loneliness and sadness that I would be experiencing. That concept has help me deal with her death. It has also helped me with many patients who have had loved ones who have died. Asking my patients to focus on where their loved ones are with all the beauty, splendor, and total glory of being with Jesus has helped many people. That concept has helped me and my patients through these difficult times. Pam had said you can't make the trip with me now but you will someday, and I will be waiting for you.

Following her funeral, I remember the boys and I standing at the back of St. Mary's Catholic Church with a dear friend, Tony Pacifico. Many months before, Tony had invited all of us to go to his ranch to deer hunt. Tony said, "The invitation is still open if you guys want to go." The boys and I had a brief discussion, and the obvious answer was Pam would insist that we go. We went home, packed up, and headed for South Texas. That night, at Tony's ranch, I wanted to sleep outside next to the campfire. Those that know me well would know this was an extremely unusual decision for me. The boys were little worried, and Hade (my policeman son) actually gave me his pistol in case any varmints should attack. It was a very peaceful night. The next day I went hunting with Treivor, my first grandson. We were walking through the woods, Treivor with his toy gun and I caring my old .30-06. We were making all sorts of noise and singing Christmas carols, and I did not expect to see any deer. I had sent the boys off hunting to "kill the big one." Treivor and I came to an opening, and I saw a large deer approximately 200 yards away. Treivor couldn't see the deer and actually said to me that he did not think there was a deer there. I ask him if I had to kill the deer to prove to him that it was there. As I raised my gun, I realized the shot was nearly impossible with a handheld rifle at 200 yards. When I pulled the trigger, the deer dropped. I've always felt that Pam asked Jesus to guide the bullet to this deer. I took pictures of Trevor sitting on the deer with my gun. That was the last deer in my hunting career.

Following Pam's death, I returned to my practice and tried to lose my sadness by staying busy. The College Station Medical Center had been purchased by a group of prior HCA investors. One of the senior people in HCA formed a new spin-off company called Triad Hospitals, Inc. I became very close to the leadership of Triad. I was chosen to be a founding member of the Physician's Leadership Group in College Station and to be on the founding group of physicians for the National Physician Leadership Group. That group had been established to develop great physician–hospital relationships and make each of their hospitals the best they could be. That group led to several more miracles in my life.

Early in 1999, I was invited to the first national group meeting in Florida. That trip made me realize how lonely it was to be with a group of physicians and their wives without Pam. It also made me realize that I would not do well by myself during the remainder of my life. Pam had realized this. We had discussed that issue before her death. She had told me I would probably find someone and that when it happened I should remarry.

Shortly after that hunting trip, I was having a phone conversation with a dear friend, Father George Henninger, a Catholic priest. He also had been Pam's very good friend. He called to check on me and invited me to come to Indianapolis, Indiana, where he was a hospital chaplain. Father Henninger has such a great personality and is such a happy person to be with, I felt it would be good to spend time with him. Since he was such a good friend of Pam's, I felt it would be good to be with him and discuss my life and future.

That was an incredible trip. When I arrived at the airport, Father George met me with a friend. He said something had come up! A dear friend had died, and he was asked to do the funeral. We had to drive to Detroit! Detroit is nowhere close to Indianapolis, Indiana. We headed out in his friend's car. If any of you have been with Father Henninger, you understand that it was one laughing matter after another. The friend was a lawyer. Father Henninger said our trip started out as one of the old jokes: "There were these three men in a car on a cold winter night. One was a priest, one a lawyer, and the third a doctor." Sometime around one or two o'clock in the morning, we decided to take turns driving so we could all take naps and continue our journey safely. We had to drive through the entire night to get to Detroit in time for the funeral. It was during Father's time to drive when the car ran out of gas in the middle of nowhere. Father Henninger said it was close to Dan Quayle's home. I'm not sure what that has to do with anything, just a Father George comment. I had only a light Texas coat, and it was quite cold outside. We were finally rescued by a Good Samaritan. We completed our trip with stomach muscles hurting because of the incredibly hilarious Father Henninger's comments on our situation. That trip helped a lot to relieve my sadness and to start out with hopes of developing "my new life." I consider that trip another great gift from God.

Cindy had been a part of our life since Chris was in the first or second grade. Pam and Cindy had become best friends. Pam and I took care of Cindy's children each night when she came to our Houston home to tutor Chris. We fought many battles to accomplish getting Chris through school. Cindy's children, Katie and Cody, became part of our family. They called us Uncle Dick and Aunt Pam. The story of Christopher is truly miraculous and is so much a part of our story it is hard to leave it out. I will touch on it only briefly with the hope that Chris and Cindy will do more justice to sharing that miracle someday.

Christopher was in approximately the third grade when Cindy had a meeting with Pam and me. She felt that he would never read properly and that we must abandon our intensive efforts to teach him to read and told us we should concentrate on his strengths and not his weaknesses. Cindy stated, "There are no disabled children. They are just differently abled." We began working with Christopher's strengths. He soon developed into being the outstanding art student in school. Many of his incredible projects are around our house today and are a testimony to this fact. There were sculptures and paintings that were incredibly good. I remember going to baseball games with the older boys. Christopher would play in the sand and sculpt Garfield characters. People would walk by in amazement since they looked like a professional sculptor had done them. Using Christopher strengths and an incredible amount of tutoring, we were able to get Christopher through high school and into college.

With the help of a friend, we were able to get Christopher into the Universe to Arkansas. Through a very complicated and incredibly interesting story, Christopher transferred to Texas A&M, made it to dental school, and graduated with honors from dental school. That complex story must be written by Christopher and Cindy. I just bring it up for you to appreciate how many years and how closely Pam and I had worked with Cindy to accomplish this goal. *Of course it was all done with the grace of God.* Our two families became one—a truly blended family.

Many men never meet the perfect woman. God has blessed me with two. As you might imagine, after Pam's death, Cindy and I fell in love and were married July 10, 1999. Some men are just not made to live alone. God blessed me with Cindy, and I was able to return to the land of the living. I believe Pam had something to do with this happening, particularly since they were best friends. When we walked out of the church after our wedding, there was a thunderstorm in the distance with three rainbows. I interpreted that God was not completely satisfied, with the thunder storm moving close, but the three rainbows were special. I knew He would lead me back to full union with His church.

Shortly after our wedding, I was asked to attend a conference on treatment of lipid disorders. We went to Colorado Springs, Colorado, and had a beautiful room at the Broadmoor Hotel. This was the first trip we made after our honeymoon vacation. We had a great time hiking around the place and really enjoyed visiting the zoo that was close by. The first night, there was a dinner for all the doctors attending the meeting. Cindy and I sat next to a couple from California. Somehow we got on the subject of spirituality in medicine. I described the Troas concept. It turned out the physician was a very spiritual man, and we had an in-depth conversation about the topic. He was the physician in charge of arranging for Grand Rounds at the University of California, Loma Linda. Grand Rounds are a weekly academic conference at all medical schools. Speakers discuss a topic of medical care or review a patient's illness in-depth for teaching. He asked if I would give a Grand Rounds at his medical school on my concepts of spirituality in medicine. His organization is a faith-based hospital and medical school, so this type of lecture would be well received. It was arranged, and I went to Loma Linda University of California in approximately April 2000 to give that talk. I prayed a lot for success, and it was accomplished. My concept was well received, as expected. A faith-based organization is on the same page that I am on and does not feel God interferes with healing, but instead helps. This supports the Troas concept I will discuss later. What are the odds of sitting down at a distant place and exchanging ideas that led to a major presentation at a major medical school? Again, I believe it had nothing to do with me but rather with God's desire to spread this concept. Dr. Hegstad learned that the first book that had started me on my spiritual journey in medicine was a book by

Taylor Caldwell called *Dear and Glorious Physician*. It is the story of Saint Luke's life. Saint Luke was a physician. My first copy was given to me by Pam in August 1974 while at Inks Lake just before I went into cardiology practice in Waco, Texas. My copy was a paperback and had fallen apart long before. Dr. Hegstad gave me a hardback copy that I had with me as I was writing this paragraph.

At that time, I was still at the College Station Medical Center. I had completed my tour of duty as leader of the Physician Leadership group and was going to my last Triad Physician Leadership national meeting. It was being held in San Francisco. Prior to Pam's death, we had been unable to make the trip to the wine country that Pam had requested. Cindy came up with the idea of having a trip to the wine country in remembrance of Pam's desire to go there. We could do that before the Physician Leadership group meeting. This was the first trip of many that Cindy arranged using computers and the Internet. It was an amazing trip!

Pam had enjoyed going up in hot air balloons. I had never done that. Cindy arranged for us to go in a hot air balloon in California. That morning was very cloudy, and the pilot of the balloon felt we would have to cancel the trip. After a while, he decided it was worth a try. It was a large basket, in which were three couples and the pilot. Shortly after takeoff I notice that the pilot was becoming uncomfortable, and I asked him if there was a problem. He said there was. We were drifting in a wrong direction, and we had to make a decision. We had two choices: come down at this time and plan the trip for another day or go up through the clouds and hope for a different wind direction that would correct our problem. He said it was against the law to go up since a balloon flies by sight alone. There are no instruments to fly without direct vision. The three couples voted and unanimously agreed to go through the clouds. Going through the clouds was quite an eerie feeling. It was cold and damp and deathly silent, except for the intermittent blasts of the flame generating the hot air for the balloon.

As we broke through the clouds, an incredible site appeared. The shadow of our balloon reflected on the clouds west of us, and the rising sun generated multiple circular rainbows around the shadow of our balloon. The pilot commented that he had never seen such a phenomenon. Cindy said that she bet Pam was tugging on Jesus's robe and asking him to create a thrilling ride. I actually took a photograph of this phenomenon, and it is somewhere in our collection of thousands of pictures.

We came down and headed for the second schedule event that day. We were going to the Mondavi Winery to have a special tour with approximately ten people. We had paid extra money for the special attention of a small group tour. When we arrived at the Mondavi Winery, we learned the other eight people had not shown up. Coincidence or God's plan? This led to a very personal tour, with our tour guide taking Cindy and I around the Mondavi vineyard. When the tour was over, she said that since there were only two of us we would have a special treat for our lunch—we would go to a special part of the location and sit next to the table where Robert Mondavi would eat lunch. Sure enough, Robert Mondavi appeared and we got to meet him, his daughter, and son. He came to our table and gave Cindy a kiss. Cindy made a pledge to never drink any wine except Mondavi wine in the future. What an incredible experience. When we left the vineyard, Cindy again commented that this was definitely Pam arranging for Jesus to make this a very special day.

That was the day that my meeting started in San Francisco. We checked into the hotel in San Francisco and had a pre-meeting cocktail party. At the cocktail party, I was asked to be on the board of directors of the National Physician Leadership Group for Triad Hospitals, Inc. Of course I accepted. That meant three more years of all-expense paid trips to wonderful places like San Francisco as well as the opportunity to become closer to the Triad Hospital organization, which meant so much to me. Cindy stated that she was now sure that Pam, through Jesus, had made these arrangements happen.

On conclusion of the meeting, Cindy and I took a walking tour through Chinatown. It was a Saturday afternoon, and we would be traveling home on Sunday. Cindy made a comment that we would not be able to go to church on Sunday. We were standing next to a Catholic church in San Francisco's Chinatown and decided to go to mass.

We were sitting in the pews when the priests walked out and stated that he was Father Robert Pinkston of the Paulist Fathers. He asked us to introduce ourselves to the person next to us. He made the comment that you never know who you might meet. I turned to Cindy in amazement! Pam had always stated that her ticket to heaven was a man named Robert Pinkston. She had met Robert when they were at the University of Texas. She was instrumental in his conversion to becoming a Catholic and, subsequently, a Catholic Paulist priest. The priest then said, "One day I met a girl while I was at the University of Texas, and that person led to me becoming a priest."

I could hardly wait till the Mass was over. As soon as it ended, I went up to Father Pinkston and said, "You do not know me, but I know you. Do you remember a girl at the University of Texas named Pam King?" He smiled and said that he did. I relayed the above recollection and stated that from the events of the past few days, it was obvious that Pam was in heaven. *What are the chances of me walking into a church in Chinatown in San Francisco and have that event occur?* Of course we thanked Jesus for allowing us to experience all the phenomena that had occurred in those past few days. I have told that story to many people, particularly those that do not believe in God. Somehow many of them still say it was just coincidental.

Two years later, I became the national president of the Triad Physician Leadership Group. As usual with many of the things in my life, I did not seek this position; it was handed to me by the grace of God. That position placed me on the national board of directors for Triad Hospitals Incorporated. That was an incredible experience and another miracle. There were many wonderful episodes connected with this position, but the episode I remember most was being trapped in an airport at Bentonville, Arkansas, where we had gone to tour a new hospital that had just opened for Triad. Going home, our flights were delayed, and I got to spend two hours with two incredible people: Gale Sayers, the famous football player with the Chicago Bears, and

Uwe Reinhardt, professor of Economics and Public Affairs at Princeton University. They were both on the board of directors of Triad with me. There was a movie written about Gale Sayers's football career and his overcoming incredible odds to return to football after a severe knee injury. The movie is Bryan's Song and was about Bryan Piccolo and his relationship with Gale. Check it out; it's great. It was incredible talking with Gale about his football career. He subsequently went back to the University of Kansas, where he had played before going to the NFL, and obtained a master's degree in computer science and developed his own computer company in Chicago. This airport experience occurred in the year 2003 or 2004. At the time, Dr. Reinhardt was helping the Chinese developed their economics. He claimed that China would be the leader in the world in a matter of a few years. It looks like he was right. I had not had time to just sit and talk with them while on the board. This was an unbelievable opportunity. Coincidence or God?

One day a patient of mine had given me two things to read. One was the Saint Faustina's autobiography regarding her encounters with Jesus. It was a very difficult read but incredible. The other was a pamphlet titled "Pieta." I will talk about it later.

Reading the book regarding Saint Faustina led to her becoming one of my heroes. Sometimes in life it is easy to go against your faith. I had done it before. That issue made me remember a conversation that I had had with Pam a couple of years prior to receiving the book. I can remember standing in the bathroom and having one of our long, in-depth conversations that were usually instigated as part of misunderstanding. I don't remember what we were talking about when I made one of the most stupid comments of my life. I'm not sure exactly how I said it, but I said something to the effect that I would never commit a serious sin. I remember feeling a shudder go through me as the words left my mouth. What I should have said was "With the grace of God, I hope I will never commit a serious sin." However, I said it the other way, as if I was in control. Remember, pride goes before a fall. I initially felt that I should leave this out of this book. I am putting it back in because of two important lessons for my grandchildren. The first important lesson is to never leave the grace of God. You must always strive to stay in a state of grace so that you will reach the ultimate goal that God has planned for you: to be in heaven with Him. Anything that gets in the way of that purpose should be avoided at all cost or, in my case, put off until better arrangements can be accomplished. The second lesson is best described through an experience I had of receiving God's forgiveness regarding my concerns. I will relay the story now.

During this time period, I had been reading the life story and autobiography of Saint Faustina. For those that are not familiar with her, it was through her vision that the concept of "Divine Mercy" became expanded. The readings are extremely tough, but I would encourage all to read it. Briefly, Saint Faustina was a nun in Poland and was a mystic. She actually predicted that Pope John Paul II would become pope many years before it actually happened. She had visions of Jesus and developed a broader understanding of His Divine Mercy. There is a famous painting that is in most Catholic churches of the crucified Jesus standing with his hands open with merciful rays coming forth from his heart, sending forgiveness to the world. The colors represent the blood and water shed during the crucifixion when the spear was thrust into His side. Through these visions, Saint Faustina expanded the concept of *trusting in the Lord*.

I had been troubled by the fact that my second marriage had taken place outside the Catholic Church. Catholic Reconciliation (confession) is a means for receiving forgiveness of sins and additional grace. Forgiveness, of course, comes through Jesus; the priest is acting as His surrogate. I had been asked to attend a training program for the lipid-lowering drug Crestor in San Francisco. While at the meeting, I hoped to see the priest I had mentioned earlier, the Paulist priest in Chinatown. I wanted to discuss my problem. On arrival at my hotel, I call the Catholic church in Chinatown and was informed that Father Pinkston was no longer there. I was very disappointed and was sitting in the hotel room by myself, praying for guidance, when I noticed church bells ringing.

I walked to the window of my room and observed that there was a church next to the hotel. The bells in its steeple were ringing. I decided to investigate further and walk to the church. When I walked into the church I discovered a huge banner of Saint Faustina's Divine Mercy painting with red and blue rays flowing from Jesus's heart. In most churches, this painting is no more than four feet by two feet. This was a banner in the center of the altar and was at least twelve feet tall! Needless to say, I felt my prayer for forgivingness had been answered. I went to confession. The poor priest was with me a long time. When our discussion was over, he gave me absolution. I felt the weight of the world was off my shoulders. That experience changed my life. Again, what are the odds regarding my reading Faustina's story of *trust in the Lord and His Divine Mercy* with my walking into a church with the twelve-foot banner depicting that mercy on the altar? In my mind, that sequence of events is *another miracle* in my life, this time demonstrating *God's forgiveness.*

The same patient that gave me the material on Saint Faustina gave me another important read. It was a little pamphlet titled "Pieta." In it are many prayers that changed my life. I recommend obtaining a copy. It is published by Divine Mercy Publications. In it I found the fifteen prayers of Saint Bridget of Sweden. After completing saying these fifteen prayers daily for one year, as Saint Bridget had been told by Jesus to do to honor the 5480 blows to His body, I started having visual problems. I had been wearing glasses since my freshman year in medical school. I began noticing I was having difficulty seeing the television screen during my procedures in the cardiac catheterization lab. I went to an Ophthalmologist friend for evaluation. When he finished, he told me the visual problem was that I no longer needed glasses! After thirty-five years of wearing glasses, my vision was 20/20! My vision has remained good, requiring only mild reading glasses recently. I am claiming this as another miracle. I believe the prayers had everything to do with it, since my vision returned following my completing the yearlong daily prayers. I subsequently made a pilgrimage to Saint Bridget's convent in Sweden and began the fifteen daily prayers for a second year from July 2010 to July 2011. I have never wanted to be one of the nine lepers who did not return to Jesus following their cure (Luke17:11–19). I have always tried to model myself after the tenth leper, who returned to thank Jesus. That is my thank you, Jesus! It is also thanks to Jesus for his help in writing this book and in my life!

While in College Station, Cindy's daughter, Katie, began college at Texas State University in San Marcus in 2002. She had an opportunity to have a year of studies at the University of Massachusetts for her second year. I had felt that my East Coast experience had helped me tremendously and therefore supported her efforts to accomplish this year at the University of Massachusetts. During spring break of 2003, we went to Stowe, Vermont, for the first time to go skiing in the east. During part of that trip we stayed at the Trapp Family Lodge. They were developing a program of "fractional ownership" of villas being built on their property. For very unclear reasons, I felt this was a good opportunity.

We returned at the end of Katie's year and spend a weekend at the Trapp Family Lodge. I had prayed extensively regarding the crazy idea of purchasing a fractional ownership of one of these villas. On picking Katie up at the University of Massachusetts, I commented to Cindy and Katie that I wanted to arrive on the Trapp property at sunset. Because of my prior faith experiences regarding sunsets, I had asked God that if He wanted me to purchase this villa, He would create an amazing sunset for us to witness. If there is a routine sunset or no sunset (it was a totally overcast day), I will leave the villa and not regret that decision. We arrived at the Trapp Family Lodge parking lot for the cross-country skiing area just at the time sunset should be occurring. Remember it was totally overcast. After sitting there for couple minutes, the sky turned an amazing red color as the sun dropped out of the clouds. It was one of the sunsets that I have learned to accept as a message from God.

The next day I began discussions for purchasing one of the "fractional ownerships" of the villas on the Trapp family property. On return home, my financial advisor/accountant and my office manager both were against me undertaking this financial burden. I, however, felt that the odds of developing that sunset we witnessed were incredibly small since all the days before and after that day were overcast and gray, and I therefore felt I had been encouraged by God to begin negotiations for acquiring the villa.

The Villa 11 has turned out to be a wonderful place for family get-togethers. I remember our first trip there. It was spring break 2004. Cindy and I were there with Katie and Cody and one of Cody's friends, Lance. The road to the villa had not been completed. We had to drive up in our rented four-wheel truck, straight up the hill in front of the villa, in a major snow storm. On walking into the villa, we said a prayer of thanksgiving to God for allowing us to have acquired such a wonderful place. As it turns out, most of this book was written while I was at the villa during multiple times over the last few years. I felt it appropriate to write this book for the glorification of God at the place he allowed us to acquire despite financial difficulties. This clearly was another blessing in my life. The necessary finances were all worked out easily. The Green Mountains of Vermont at the Trapp Family Lodge Villas turned out to be a perfect place to write this book of my life.

Back in College Station, I had some problems working with my partners. Issues arose at times because of my temper but probably more often because of our age difference and our different ideas of where we needed to head to maintain our lead in cardiology. In retrospect, all of these issues were meaningless but at the time seemed important. As I was getting older, I needed a more guaranteed and less stressful way to arrange for time off. I was talking about options of becoming an employed physician for the Med (College Station Medical Center) and starting another group. The Med and I had recruited a cardiologist to work with me. That had turned into a disaster. The person we had hired was well trained but a total mismatch for me and our community.

One day on driving to work, I witnessed another incredible scene. This time it was a sunrise. It was so beautiful! I jokingly said to Jesus in a prayer, "What do you have in store for me today?"

That morning, a good friend named George Rodgers called me about a mutual patient. He was the president of Austin Heart at the time. I must have been having a particularly bad day with Marcel and Mario and vented a little with George. I had always felt close to George. I had known his father for many years through a prestigious group the Texas Club of Internists. George's father had been a good referring physician to my Houston cardiology group. George had also become a member of the Texas Club of Internists. He had been a fellow in cardiology training with our group in Houston. We had tried to recruit him to stay in Houston, but he had gone to Austin and, as expected, had done very well.

In our phone conversation, he said, "Why don't you come and go into practice with us at Austin Heart?" He felt all of my issues could be solved there. In fact, he stated he was strongly considering leaving Austin Heart for a job offer for some type of medical lab company. He said it would be easier to tell the group that he was leaving if another experienced cardiologist was coming to join Austin Heart. I agreed we should visit more and scheduled a meeting in Austin on Sept 19, 2004. I thought it was interesting to meet on this day, since September 19 was Boppie's (Pam's father's) birthday. He had always wanted me to practice in Austin. As mentioned, he had passed away several years earlier.

That meeting went very well, and it was decided I should return to meet several other key members of Austin Heart. While in that meeting, George suggested I visit with Matt Phillips, who was with Austin Heart in the Killeen, Texas, office. The phone conversation was incredible. After that one conversation, I said to George, "I need to meet that guy." It was arranged for me to go to Killeen to meet him. The Killeen office of Austin Heart was working with Metroplex Hospital administration to find someone to start an interventional program without surgical backing. It would be in partnership with Austin Heart and Metroplex each paying 50 percent of the cardiologist salary. On the night of our meeting, there was a total eclipse of the moon. I'm not sure how that fits in, but it is interesting that we made the decision to go to the Austin Heart office in Killeen, Texas, as Cindy and I were watching the total eclipse of the moon. It is also interesting that the first picture I noticed on one of the walls at Metroplex hospital was the classic painting of Jesus holding the hand of the surgeon performing an operation. I did not want to go to a place where Jesus was not welcome. That painting made me feel good about my decision.

This series of events led to my leaving College Station, where I had practiced for ten years. If you recall, the sequence of events that lead to that move began with another beautiful natural event (the sunrise in College Station described earlier). That move changed my life in a very spiritual way. I will now begin relating the next phase of my life. Since these spiritual events occurred while living in Salado, Texas, I will call them the Salado Years. For a long time, I truly wondered if this was a move God wanted me to make or if I was doing it for other reasons. As the story develops, you will see it was the most important move of my spiritual life and of my relationship with God.

CHAPTER 13

The Salado Years

The Salado part of my life was complicated and is difficult to write about in chronologic order, considering there were two areas of my life that were progressing simultaneously. These were the medical and the spiritual considerations regarding the Troas Health Care concept. Each of these areas has a significant correlation with the other, so that these two areas are interwoven. I will start off with the professional side of things, since the spiritual side with Troas Health Care resurfaced after my move to Salado.

On March 1, 2005, I began working for Austin Heart in Killeen, Texas. I had been appointed as chief of cardiology at Metroplex hospital. I had been recruited to start an interventional (stents and coronary angioplasty) program without surgical backup, a pioneer consideration in 2005. At the time I started this, very few programs were doing interventions without surgical backup. It was contrary then to mainstream recommendations and many were very critical of this policy. To be sure that everything would go well, I worked diligently to develop policies and procedures to ensure patient safety. Helicopter backup was necessary to consider transport of failed procedures requiring urgent bypass surgery. I had never before had to check the weather report prior to an intervention. Now emergency transfer would be potentially required, so reviewing the weather report each morning was going to be a new consideration. When I was in Houston and in College Station, if an intervention required urgent surgical backup, it would take an average of one hour from the time the surgeon was called until the patient was in the operating room with an open chest. I made several "dry run" helicopter trips to determine if this was possible. In fact, with the helicopter crews on standby and all appropriate preparations made, this could be accomplished in less than an hour from Killeen, Texas. We therefore proceeded. I believe it was in October 2005 when we did the first coronary intervention (stent placed in a coronary) without surgical backup. It was close to my sixty-fourth birthday. Everything went well, and our interventional program was started. We recruited a second interventional cardiologist, Randy McCollough, to help so we could start doing 24/7 coverage for opening acute coronary artery occlusions.

We were trying to build a partnership and joint venture cardiology program between Austin Heart and Metroplex hospital. Metroplex kept adding delays to our negotiations. One day we found out that Metroplex was simultaneously talking with our main competition, Scott & White. They partnered with Scott & White and our plans took a nose dive. I was relieved of my position approximately July 2007. Metroplex and Scott & White developed an "our way or the highway" plan. If we wanted to stay in the area and continue to care for our patients, we would need a second hospital. The non–Scott & White physicians began discussions regarding the possibility of

The Road From Troas

building a second hospital. After almost five years, we opened that second hospital.

There were many months of considering all our options for all the non–Scott & White practicing physicians at Metroplex. We formed a group called Killeen Investment Partners. We had hoped to build a hospital as a joint venture between the physicians and the hospital, but government rules and regulations changed that. When it looked like our plan was going to fail, I decided to call Denny Shelton. I had worked with Denny while I was in College Station. Through Triad Physician Leadership Group, I had become the national president of that group (another gift from God) and was therefore on the board of directors for Triad Hospitals, Inc., as I described earlier. When I explained the situation that approximately sixty unhappy physicians were looking for a new home, he said, "We'll give it a look." I do not remember the date of that conversation; it was probably late 2010. At that time, Denny was the chairman of the board for the new company Legacy Hospital Partners, Inc. (LHP). Their goal was to build and manage hospitals, as Triad had done. The story of what happened to Triad and how Legacy was formed is very interesting but not appropriate for this book. I believe our official meeting with the Legacy group occurred around January 2011. The new hospital ground breaking for a $100 million project was in April 2011. Most of the due diligence for building a new hospital had been done in the prior three years of planning, so the project moved at lightning speed. With God's grace, the new hospital was completed in record-breaking time. This hospital had no physician ownership. We were very happy, however, to have a new home.

The next two blessings occurred in rapid sequence. The first is that the new Seton Medical Center Harker Heights opened for patient care June 18, 2012! The second miracle relates to that event. I was asked to be the chairman of the board of trustees for this new hospital. Yet again, I did not seek the position but was just asked if I would do it. Since my College Station years, I have always looked at these opportunities as gifts from God. By accepting these unforeseen adventures, I felt was following God's plan. Thank you, Jesus, for all you have done for me. I know there is nothing I can do to repay all the blessings. I just want to be able to follow where you are leading me and publicly express my gratitude for all these blessings.

Starting a new hospital from the ground up is quite interesting. To begin with, no one is on the nonexistent medical staff. There are no bylaws or criteria for acceptance to the medical staff and no organization to develop these crucial things. It took a lot of effort to accomplish all the necessary work, but with the help of God, we were able to succeed. A new office building was also built. We moved to our new professional home in September 2012. It felt good to leave Metroplex after they betrayed our trust after all of our hard work. I had forgiven them, but it just felt so good to be at the new hospital that truly wanted us there. Being involved with all this—from the initial thought of a new hospital in July 2007 to its opening June 18, 2012—was a significant part of my life for those five years.

I would like to now turn to the spiritual part of my life during this same period of our Salado adventure. So many things happened, it is hard to chronologically put it together. There were three main areas of change and growth. The first was finding the right church for me, an answer to Cindy's prayer. The second was developing a better prayer life with a closer relationship with Jesus and with the multiple saints I have come to know and love. This also includes my relationship with Max, my guardian angel. The third is how I came to feel the Troas concept needed to be reactivated.

Finding a Church for Me and Cindy

During the first five years in Salado, I tried multiple churches. I kept searching—for what, I'm not sure. I had finally settled on St. Stephen's in Salado, mostly because of its close proximity and the pastor, Father Charlie. Through St. Stephen's Catholic Church, we met a couple, Rick and Denice Thomssen. We met them at the church festival when we ended up in a bidding war over some items that were being auctioned. We had a great time and felt like we became good friends on that single occasion. We have subsequently spent a lot of time with them at their chapel that they build on their little property. Father Charlie passed away before Rick's Chapel had been completed. Rick had been involved with starting a group that became known as the "Tuesday Night Mass Club." Rick got Cindy and I involved with "TNMC." We began going to Mass each Tuesday night and dinner following that Mass. We got to know several of the people at the St. Stephen's parish.

Shortly after our arrival in Salado, Cindy became good friends with Tyler Fletcher, who had built the little Episcopal Chapel for St. Joseph in Salado. Cindy became very involved with that group, and as a results of that, we had many happy occasions at the St. Joseph Chapel. A friend of Tyler's is a Catholic priest, Father Jamie Misko. We had met him a few times at Tyler's home. He ended up being assigned to Christ the King Catholic Church in Belton, Texas. Because of our relationship, I decided to go to his first Mass at Christ the King Catholic Church, which I believe was sometime in the summer of 2010. I was overwhelmed by his magnetism and excellent sermons. I decided to make that church my parish. In the fall of 2010, Father Jamie asked me to be involved with an organization called That Man Is You. I began coming to the meetings, which met at 6:00 a.m. every Wednesday morning. That organization was created to develop Christian male leadership. Through that group, I met many members of the parish at Christ the King and began to feel that it was my new spiritual home.

Developing a Better Prayer Life

I feel some concern over discussing my prayer life, since I believe that prayer is a private matter and should not be made a spectacle. I remember Jesus's caution about keeping it private. Therefore, I share this reluctantly, but I feel it is essential to illustrate how my prayer life has helped me realize the means necessary to reach my goal to try to get to heaven and complete what I feel Jesus is asking me to do.

Living in Salado resulted in my needing to drive to Killeen, Texas, each day. The drive took thirty to forty minutes each way. I began saying a series of prayers during my commute rather than listening to the radio. These prayers became a part of my daily life and resulted in a much closer relationship with Jesus. I would usually include a Rosary and the Saint Joseph prayer (the one found in the 1500s, usually part of a nine day novena). I would pray for whoever I felt needed help, with a separate Saint Joseph prayer for each person. I would also say a part of Saint Faustina's chaplet. Her "Trust in the Lord" became ever present in my life. I have a mental list of fifteen priest whom I pray for at least five days a week. At least ten years ago, a cardiac catheterization nurse named Tony gave me the prayer of Jabez. I began saying it each day. It goes like this: "Bless me, Lord. Expand my ministry. Let me feel your touch. Deliver me from evil so I cause no pain." I would say the "Jesus prayer" whenever I was walking in the hospital halls or had a free moment driving the car. For those that don't know it, it comes from the book *The Pilgrim*, which was by an unknown author who was probably Russian Orthodox. It goes like this: "Lord Jesus Christ, Son of God, have mercy on me, a sinner." You can easily develop a mantra with saying this over and over, as I frequently did. I found you could time the words with steps of walking or climbing stairs. These devotions made my day and the daily trip to and from go Killeen much faster. I began to also feel much closer to Saint Mary and Saint Joseph. There were many prayers that I saw answered through these intercessory prayers. I also read *The Story of a Soul* by Saint Thérèse of Lisieux, the biography of Saint Faustina, Saint Teresa of Ávila's autobiography, and Augustine of Hippo. These readings had a profound influence on my life. One of the most influential books was the book *Mother Angelica*. The story of her faith and how she built the EWTN radio/TV network gave me hope about the Troas concept. Each morning I would pray for the attitude of Thérèse Lisieux, faith of Angelica, the trust of Faustina, and for Devine Wisdom. The book *Catholicism* by Reverend Robert Barron as well as his video series were all absorbed in 2011–2012. The drive to Killeen, Texas, allowed me to pass by a Catholic church that had a twenty-four-hour-a-day adoration chapel. I frequently would stop for a visit to say a brief hello to Jesus and thank Him for all He had done for me. These visits in the adoration chapel allowed me to become even closer to Jesus and feel His presence. All of these prayers were good, but I never was able to reach even the Level II of prayer life discussed by Teresa of Ávila. I still have a long way to go!

Meeting My Guardian Angel

In September 2010, Cindy and I were invited to visit my best friend from high school, Pat Melton. We had invited Pat and his wife, Mary Lena, to our place in Vermont the year before. On this occasion, we were invited to their home in New Mexico. During that stay, we took a train ride on the Chama, New Mexico, to Antonito, Colorado, narrow gauge railway. It was a beautiful, cool, and completely clear day. Because of some issued with the train track leaving Chama, we were bused to the Colorado town to start the trip that would end back in New Mexico. The train company encouraged us to walk between cars and take pictures of the scenery. The train had left the Colorado train station and had climbed up the mountain to an elevation of approximately 8000 feet. It was mostly desert, but there were a few small ponderosa pines that were appearing. I was looking out one way taking a picture, and Cindy was standing at the intersection between two cars taking a picture of me. When I turned around, Cindy was gone! The gate on her side had apparently opened

The Road From Troas

while we were going around a steep curve. I ran to her side of the train and saw her rolling down the hill. I couldn't believe my eyes! She had fallen off the train! I made the instantaneous decision to jump after her, since I was fearful she may have broken her neck and would need someone to stabilize her. Without telling anyone, I said a quick prayer and jumped off the train. I knew I had to be running very fast when I hit the ground, since the train was moving fifteen to twenty miles an hour at that time. As I jumped, I clearly felt someone supporting me. I landed in a full run heading in the same direction that the train was going. They were cactus plants, rocks, and a steep slope as well as the railroad ties extending from under the tracks, but I never fell or stumbled. I had absolutely no injuries. I turned around and headed back down the railroad track, running alongside the train in the opposite direction so I could reach Cindy. As I ran I signaled to stop the train, but I was not sure anyone saw me. By the time I got to Cindy, she had hopped up on one leg and was a standing there a bloody mess. I knew she was okay when the first thing out of her mouth was, "Where's my iPhone?" I dusted her off, as best I could, and we both watched the train chug away. I found Cindy's iPhone, but neither my phone or her phone had any signal! We were in the middle of the high mountain desert with no water and were not sure anybody had seen us exit the train. After what seemed to be a long time, we heard the train chugging backward toward us.

When the train arrived, people helped me get Cindy back onboard. We got her to the part of the train that had a refreshment stand. I got a couple bottles of water and started washing off her lacerated areas. Two EMS people arrived and began helping us; they were also passengers on the train and on vacation. They began opening an ice pack that required squeezing for the pack to turn cold. On squeezing the pack it exploded, its fluid going into both my eyes and Cindy's eyes. I began turning the bottles of water on our faces to wash out our eyes. After several bottles, things were better and we could see. We were given the option of calling in a helicopter or continuing on the train a short distance to where a pickup could bring us to an ambulance. Cindy seemed completely stable with no fractures, and so we chose the pickup. Her bleeding had stopped, but she was developing a huge hematoma in her calf. On arrival to the spot where the pickup was waiting, we carried Cindy to the pickup. The pickup began a long, bumpy trip down to a state highway, where the ambulance was waiting for us. In the ambulance, the nurse attendant fell on top of Cindy while we were going around the first curve. Thankfully, Cindy did not sustain any additional injuries with this heavy nurse falling on top of her. We arrived in the small hospital in Colorado. They placed Cindy in the emergency room bed, and we waited a minute or two before the physician in attendance arrived.

The door to our emergency room open, and the physician came in using a motorized wheelchair with nasal oxygen in place! It turns out that he had been in a major car accident a few years earlier and was a paraplegic. After examining Cindy's right side, he motored around the foot of her bed to examine her left side. All the cables and IV tubing were caught in the motorized wheelchair, and as he reached the foot of her bed the whole monitoring system and IV fell over, crashing to the floor with a loud noise. I heard the physician whisper to the nurse, "Do we have another monitor?" The nurse said, "No." The monitor was irretrievably broken. Cindy was then given tetanus toxoid and antibiotic. At that point she began feeling very bad and developed severe hypertension, with blood pressure well over 220/120, and began having visual distortions. This blood pressure was followed by an altered mental status and a feeling of impending doom. Things gradually settled down, and the physician said, "You will need to be admitted." I whispered in Cindy's ear, "We're getting out of here."

My friend Pat and his wife had retrieved their car in Chama, New Mexico, and were at the hospital waiting for us. We were helped out to the car and got Cindy in the backseat. Cindy had asked for a drink of water and was leaning against the door when it was opened from the outside. Cindy almost fell out of the truck! I happened to be sitting next her and caught her as the door opened. We were very happy to leave that place. We drove to a beautiful rented house in Taos, New Mexico, where Cindy recovered for the next two days.

My jump from the train was an incredible experience. I had absolutely no injury, not even a sprained ankle. I felt certain that my guardian angel had guided me safely to the ground. I began to pray that I would know my guardian angel's name. Several weeks later, I learned in a dream that his name is Max. Max and I have always been together, but I now know his name and frequently talk to him. I began to wonder how many times Max had saved my life in the past. I began recalling multiple episodes in my life where I had been spared. I will not list them all, but they include near car wrecks, falling through ice on a lake, a near drowning with three of my boys, as well as many others episodes.

Reactivation of Troas

At this time, I was attending weekly services at Christ the King Catholic Church with Father Misko. One Sunday, Father caught me as I was entering church. He told me a program was starting that I had to be a part of: That Man Is You. The program began at Christ the King Catholic Church in the fall of 2010. It followed the format of a brief video lecture done by its founder, Steve Bollman, followed by a thirty-minute discussion of what had been presented. During those discussions, I began to feel comfortable enough to talk about how much God had blessed me, to discuss some of my close relationships with the saints that I had developed, and even to tell them about Max. One morning during one of those discussions in early 2012, the question asked in the presentation was, "Have you ever been asked to do something by our Lord?" During the discussion that followed, I told my story of why I left Houston, Texas. I related the recurrent dreams about the white horses and the nun with the large white hat. I related the stories of finding our house in College Station and selling our house in Houston and my feelings that for some reason Jesus had called me to leave my comfortable Houston surroundings and come to College Station. I talked about how that move had changed my life and led me to become more open about my Christianity in my practice of medicine. I told them the Troas story.

During the discussion, one of the men asked me if I knew what the Sister of Charity nun by the white fence had to do with my decision. I had just answered that I did not know, when the man sitting next to me said, "I know the answer! The nun was a Sister of Charity, and you have been involved with developing the new Seton Catholic hospital. That's the relationship!" For those of you that do not know, Seton Medical Center Austin is run by the Sisters of Charity. In past years, they wore the characteristic large white winged hats characterized in the TV show *The Flying Nun*. Pam and I had been involved with them during our college years.

Following the morning meeting, I felt compelled to discuss the Troas concept with Father Jamie. I invited him to dinner at an Italian restaurant in Temple, Texas, where I had reserved the restaurant's small wine cellar so I could talk about the Troas concept in private. I wanted to tell him what had happened that week in That Man Is You and how it had compelled me to reactivate my thoughts regarding Troas, which had been dormant for eight years. I felt that I needed to talk with our bishop, since I believed Troas would need the support of a large religious group for nationwide and possibly worldwide health care organization.

I wanted to discuss the issue first with Father Jamie to see if he felt I was crazy to put all these events together and if it would be reasonable to discuss these events with Bishop Joe Vasquez regarding developing a spiritual-based health care system that was "completely out of the box." You see, during that time the Catholic Church had come under fire by President Obama with his HHS mandate requiring all institutions to provide birth control, sterilizations, and abortions to all people with all insurance companies. I felt that the Catholic hospital system, which included Seton hospital, might be an organization that would be interested in the concept of a group of physicians that would provide excellent healthcare and include a spiritual basis in their practice of medicine. In order for this to happen, these physicians and the Catholic hospitals would need to leave Medicare and other insurance companies, a revolutionary concept! Father Jamie told me that when I had put my ideas together in a more concrete form, he would help arrange for my visit with the bishop. For unclear reasons, I believed I also needed to discuss this with Cardinal Timothy Dolan, who was president of the US Conference of Catholic Bishops at that time. I felt that I knew Cardinal Dolan from listening to Catholic radio. To provide health care without Medicare, we would need a hospital system willing the leave the system with us. The pressure created by the HHS mandate seemed to put everything together! My son Trey had said, "God tells us what He wants, sometimes long before it happens," i.e., we learn the "what" long before the "when." I felt that "the when" was now. I felt I knew why the Sister of Charity nun was in my dream!

This occurred during Lent 2012. As part of Lent, I was attending Tuesday evening Mass at Christ the King so that Cindy and I could attend an incredible series by Reverend Robert Barron on *Catholicism*. The next Tuesday night following the discussion at That Man Is You, I went to Mass with Cindy at Christ the King with plans to go to the Reverend Barron's lecture and a talk by Father Misko following. The first reading at that Mass was from the Book of Numbers, when Moses lifts up the bronze snake on a staff to save the people from dying from their snakebites (Numbers 21:4–9). I felt that it was rather curious that it was the same Scripture verses that we had used in developing the logo for Troas. That evening during the presentation by Reverend Barron, he discussed the importance of Troas in the spread of Christianity to Europe. In Father Jamie's discussion following the presentation, he said, "I was thinking of you when Reverend Barron started talking of Troas." As a result of those overwhelming encounters, I called my oldest son, Trey, and ask him to begin working on reactivating our thoughts regarding the Troas concept. He felt we should do some type of retreat to clarify our thoughts. The very next week at the meeting of That Man Is You, one of the men sitting in my group made the comment that he would like for me to attend the next ACTS spiritual retreat. He had no idea of the thoughts I had been having. This was all a little overwhelming, since I had always felt that before launching into a serious spiritual endeavor we should do some type of spiritual retreat. I signed up for that retreat and called and asked Trey to attend it with me so we could begin discernment regarding the future of the Troas concept.

CHAPTER 14

The Troas Concept

Similar to a calling to be a priest, I feel I am now called by God to develop a new health care system for all His people. The concept has developed over many years with the help of my son Trey, as I have described. I can no longer ignore my feelings regarding an effort to save the profession I love.

We have named this new concept Troas Health Care because it directs medical care in a different direction from where it is currently heading. The HHS mandate fits with the urgent need I feel to pursue our vision.

I believe the bishops of the United States need an alternative to deal with the multiple financial and ethical problems that are developing in our current health care system. The issues have become so intense that I feel the time to consider an alternative is now.

Here are the characteristics of the Troas concept:

1. It is a totally new system that is spiritually based and delivers hospital and office care.

The Road From Troas

2. It believes and openly states that the concept of the Supreme Being is present and guides health care workers in the delivery of compassionate health care.
3. It believes we must invoke His help in the care of all patients.
4. It believes in the old concept that health care is not an individual right but the obligation of all health care professionals to use their God-given talents to care for all His people—irrespective of their financial means—and that the patients also have an equal obligation to follow the medical recommendations to the best of their ability.
5. It will help motivate all health care workers to love their patients and develop a love of the process of delivering health care more than the financial gains that are a part of our profession.
6. It excludes payment by all insurance companies except for catastrophic health care expense (+/-$25,000). "Crisis" insurance would be necessary.
7. It will develop an efficiently managed system that will prevent waste and spending.
8. It will document superior medical care by following and acting upon outcomes data.
9. It will need to be a nationwide system, and hopefully a worldwide network, so all patients can find easy access to excellent health care. The Catholic hospital system could accomplish this because of its multiple current locations throughout the world. It would encourage all religious health care organizations to work together to accomplish these goals using these common principles.

10. It will be financed mostly by donations. Large church organizations function on donations alone; I feel the system will be financially stable on donations. If people are not paying health care premiums, they would be more likely to donate to this type of system. If God wants it to happen, money will not be the problem. Overwhelming problems have been overcome by faith, demonstrated with stories of Saint Francis and Mother Teresa of Calcutta. It will take faith and a miracle, but you remember, I believe in miracles.
11. It will be a system that accepts all patients irrespective of their insurance coverage or financial status. In fact, this system hopes to eliminate the need for health insurance.
12. It would not bill patients. Troas would develop a concept of "pay what you think the service is worth." There would be no "free care." All patients would be asked to contribute something, but all types of contributions would be considered equal, e.g., time helping the organization, money to contribute to the success of the organization, or prayers if unable to do either of the former.
13. It will develop a training program for young physicians and a medical school founded on these concepts. This system would focus on excellence in medical care with an emphasis on spiritual and psychological needs of patients and their families. Compassionate care for all would be the goal.
14. It would develop a training system that would work to reduce the cost of medical education so that young physicians would not acquire such incredible debt during their training. The current system of education

results in such high debt that young physicians are driven to acquire immediate financial reward to repay this debt.

15. It would recruit older physicians who are upset with the current system of regulations and intrusion of the sacred patient–physician relationship they experienced in the past. These physicians love the practice of medicine but have become discouraged by all the government and health care insurance company involvement in their lives, which has attempted to destroy the God-given patient–physician relationship. It would recruit physicians who have a desire to save the profession that we all love. In many respects, this would be missionary medicine in the USA.

16. It would give patients coming to this type of system excellent, compassionate care with less concern regarding finances. Because of this, malpractice rates would be substantially lower and thus reduce the cost of medical care.

17. It would have decreased expenses with no government or insurance company regulations. A few examples would be the elimination of the planned computer requirements and the current very complicated system of billing. This would allow the delivery of health care at a lower cost.

18. It would develop a simplified coding system using the indexes of the leading textbooks of internal medicine, pediatrics, obstetrics-gynecology, preventive medicine/public health, and surgery so disease processes and treatment plans could be followed using the reference textbook rather than codes derived purely for financial

gain. Just imagine selecting a diagnosis and being able to read about it at the same time!
19. It would have the attitude of Mother Teresa: "It is not how much you do, but how much love you put in the doing."

CHAPTER 15

The New Job: Three in One

At this point in my life, I felt compelled to do something regarding the development of the Troas concept. In April 2013, I began submitting copies of my book to publishers. At that time the book was entitled *An Ethical Will and Testament* by Richard Cashion. I submitted copies to the Ignatius Press and Loyola Press. I also wrote a letter to Pope Francis in August 2013 and sent it with a copy of my book before this current revision. In fact, I even had hopes that the pope might call me, as he had done for others. We had arranged to go to Rome on a Christ the King pilgrimage, and I had hopes that somehow the pope might contact us. We were in the thousands of people for his weekly audience on October 2, 2013. In those days, I was obsessed with pushing forward with the concept of Troas with everything I could do. I don't think I realized that God didn't need any help from me. If He wanted it to develop, it would happen without any help from me.

Fortunately, around that time I became very involved with ACTS Ministry. Over the next two years, I diverted my energies to the ACTS Ministry. I began participating in ACTS retreats and have been to five ACTS retreats as of 2015. I became very committed to the concept of ACTS Ministry. This helped distract my compulsion to push the concept of Troas Health Care and not much has happened since that time.

In one of the recent ACTS retreats, I was told by Joe Ramos, an ACTS brother, to put Jesus in the driver's seat and that I should ride "shot gun." Several of my closest friends and my wife, Cindy, also suggested I was trying to make things happen rather than letting Jesus work in his time. There were other changes that lead to the belief I would someday complete the development of Troas Health Care, this time on Jesus's time.

I was able to return to the Christian Medical and Dental Society for my planned ten year follow-up lecture regarding Troas. You may recall that first lecture is where God told me "Don't you know I did all this for you." One of my sons, Cody, had his film crew there, and the lecture was filmed. It was recorded digitally to be placed on a future website. The lecture received few comments, but I was pleased it had been filmed by some real pros for use on the future website.

For unclear reasons, the entire film was lost! The forty-minute digital recording had been planned so it would allow continuous presentation from multiple projections and had been filmed from three different directions. This very professional approach was completed with hopes that all had gone well. However, the entire recording was lost. I was convinced it was a work of the devil.

At that time, I was very discouraged. Two attempts at publishing my book were turned down. I still hadn't heard from the pope. I had been assured that his office received three copies of my book. My website for Troas was finally completed by Cody and Heath. It is troashealthcare.com. I felt it was quite good, but there were still some changes made. Despite all this, I patiently await with faith that all will happen in God's time, not mine.

In the summer of 2013, I took an offer from Austin Heart for early retirement. By notifying Austin Heart of a planned retirement in December 2014, they would allow me to work full-time without expense. That amounted to a significant increase in my income if everything continued the same. However, with the word of my retirement spreading and a new physician being recruited to take my place, it became obvious that the increased efforts to complete my retirement would not be accomplished on the planned retirement date December 31, 2014.

I had been hopeful I would be able to spend 100 percent of my time working on Troas. However, financial concern raised its ugly head, and I began to think of other options. In the fall of 2014, a very good friend of mine, Lewis Raney, called me regarding a position opening up at the Temple Veterans' Medical Center for a full-time cardiologist. I was faced with a great dilemma and needed help with discernment.

At the same time, the new priest at St. Stephen's Catholic Church, Father Aloy, began making efforts to recruit me back to that parish to be involved with contributing to the development of a new Catholic church in Salado, Texas. Father Misko had left Christ the King Church and had been reassigned to Austin, Texas. The new priest at Christ the King, Father Kim, was outstanding, but I felt called to help Father Aloy build the church in my home community of Salado, Texas.

Father Aloy had been told by several parishioners that I must be a good fund raiser since I had helped build Seton hospital in Harker Heights. Saint Stephen's needed some additional help raising money to furnish the new church in Salado. I felt it would be nice to have Father Aloy over for dinner and explain how we had acquired the funds to build Seton hospital. It was not due to any fund raising abilities on my part.

He came over for dinner sometime in the fall of 2014. I explained that the initial $100 million needed to start building Seton Medical Center Harker Heights was arranged with one phone call to Denny Shelton as described earlier.

I told Father Aloy that I was not a good fund raiser, I just knew some good people. God had allowed me to make the right phone call at the right time; that's all there was to it. I asked Father Aloy to help me in my discernment regarding the issue of going to work for the Veteran's Hospital. That would compete with my concept of developing Troas Health Care.

Being a veteran of the Vietnam War time myself, I had been very interested in working with the Wounded Warrior Program and veterans in general. Going to work for the Veterans' Medical Center would give me an opportunity to help our needy veterans and also relieve a need I'd had to get involved with an organization helping soldiers. Father Aloy needed some help with building the church. If I went to work for the VA, I would have less time to help him but would have more income to help financially with St. Stephen's. Without a second thought, Father Aloy said I need to do both: help build St. Stephen's Church and go to work for the VA. He said, "God will give you time to help develop Troas."

It is a really big job ... really three jobs; however, with prayer and God's help, I'll do all three. I have been financially supporting St. Stephen's Catholic Church and have become more involved there. I've accepted a full-time cardiology position at the Temple Veterans' Medical Center. I am continuing to look for time to work on the Troas Health Care concept. I have been spending time on weekends working on the Troas concept and completing rewriting this book.

In reviewing my life, I realized my experiences have provided me with a unique opportunity to discuss all types of medical practice. I have been in practice in an academic setting. I have started a solo practice and grew it into a complete cardiology program that included cardiac interventions and heart surgery. This included the development a small group practice as part of that deal. I then became part of a large group practice, Austin Heart. Initially, it was privately owned by the doctors. It was quite a large group, with forty-five to fifty cardiologists in approximately ten cities. It subsequently was sold to the Hospital Corporation of America, and I became an employee of that organization. I had started an interventional program without surgical backup at Metroplex hospital for Austin Heart. When conflicts developed over the sale of that facility to Scott & White, a fierce competitor of ours, a group developed in the Killeen area to consider our options. It was either become a Scott & White physician or leave the area. I therefore became involved with building a new hospital in Harker Heights that was accomplished and is doing well. I retired from Austin Heart December 31, 2014 and have become a part of the Veterans Hospital system as a government employee. Therefore, I have been involved with the practice of medicine in almost every type of practice possible. This unique background gives me some insight into the underlying problems confronting our healthcare system today.

I initially started this book to provide a mechanism to share my life with my fifteen grandchildren—at least at this time there are only fifteen—but it's also for any future grandchildren that have not arrived yet. In writing this book over a number of years, issues have developed in the practice of medicine that I felt needed redirection. The Troas concept, I believe, was given to me by God, and I feel compelled to share this concept with the world. I now will begin to focus on what I feel is the real reason for writing this book: to develop a better health care system for all. The extensive background I have provided will help readers understand how I arrived at this concept through being involved in all different types of medical practice and why I feel the idea came from God. By seeing the influence of God in my life, I believe it gives some credence as to where the concept came from and who I am.

A majority of people have become distressed with the problems in health care delivery today. There seems to be a common thread of disapproval and distrust in all forms of medical practice. I believe there is a common problem that has led to the downfall of medicine: the removal of God from the practice of medicine. God was eliminated to remain "politically correct."

I have taken care of the poorest of poor at Boston City Hospital and the wealthiest in the world at the Methodist Hospital in Houston, Texas. I am now dealing with issues in a federal health care system, the Veterans Administration, and treating our wounded warriors. I was the son of a physician and nurse before government and health insurance companies stole our precious physician–patient relationship. I have lived through these changes and see the devastation government involvement and insurance company regulation is causing.

There is a common thread dealing with all patients, whether dealing with the pathos of poverty or the wealthy of the upper class. All sick people are looking for relief of their medical pain or problems. When I see someone, for example, with a myocardial infarction (heart attack), they are all the same regardless of finances, religious preferences, or no spirituality at all. All they want is to receive effective medical care of the highest quality. Their background is equalized when they're lying in bed with a life-threatening illness. The problem comes in providing efficient, excellent, affordable, and personalized care. Each of them want a system that will provide the best of care for their problem.

To remain "politically correct" and not force God on patients, I believe we need to start an organization that is so overtly God centered that people will choose this organization because of that belief and not be offended by that belief. This type of organization would follow the belief that God wants us to develop a caring organization that will provide excellent encounters for all people who need to have access to healing. I believe that the concept of excellence in a loving, caring environment, with no concern about finances, religious beliefs, or lack of any spiritual connections at all, will stimulate people to support this type of organization through their voluntary contributions. People would be seen without having to present an insurance card and would be asked questions related only to their health care. Since these people would not have purchased expensive health insurance policies, they would have money to contribute to the development of this concept. In other words, they could contribute to an organization willing to provide excellent care without the demand of insurance coverage. It would then make sense to "pay what you think the service is worth." I believe people would be so excited to receive excellent care without insurance, they would be generous in supporting this concept. The cost of providing care would dramatically decrease with the reduced need for expensive computer systems created predominantly for billing. In a cash only system, no time would be wasted trying to match the service rendered with one of the 14,000+ codes just implemented by our government. Since the Troas concept would be financially independent from government and health insurance payments, there would not be any complex encounters to document the level of service. If we are not under government control, there would be no need to waste time learning the new very complex billing system known as ICD 10. This would eliminate the expensive education process to teach all health care workers this new coding process. These few suggestions would result in substantial savings in time and expense.

What I see is that physicians and medical organizations have become so concerned regarding following rules and regulations that the front lines of health care have suffered. These rules and regulations are mostly related to receiving payments from the government or health insurance companies. Therefore, the actual care of patients takes a backseat. Over the past ten years, I have had to spend at least 50 percent of my time satisfying regulations and billing codes. We even have to take courses to be able to bill correctly! How does this help improve patient care? Too much emphasis is placed on the insurance forms—whether governmental or commercial. This has led to the concept that if the forms are filled out correctly, all is well. We have a serious physician shortage and a large backlog of patients in the United States that need to be seen in a timely fashion. It seems time would be better spent dealing with direct patient care and instead of satisfying regulations, done mostly for payment.

What we need is a group that is so concerned about what God wants that there is no need for rules or regulations. They will do the right thing for the right reasons. The group will be driven by what is absolutely needed for great patient care and not on correctly filled out insurance forms that lead to financial gain or the development of one's ego. This organization will live on the fruits of the Spirit: love, joy, peace, patients, kindness, generosity, faithfulness, gentleness, and self-control. In the current practice of medicine there is no emphasis on these fruits of the Spirit. More time is spent on justifying criteria for billing and compliance with regulations than on the things that really matter in developing great medical care for the *right reasons*. The Troas concept would allow more time for direct patient care and allow health care workers an opportunity to demonstrate the fruits of the Spirit.

You might be concerned that this system would have no documentation regarding the quality of care and that some health care workers would take advantage of that. Sure, there are bad apples in every basket. To prevent poor health care delivery, this system would police its own by making sure outcomes and patient satisfaction were superior in all respects. Let me remind you, the physicians of the United States built the best system of medicine in the world prior to the current interference by the government and health insurance regulations. Where do we stand now? Most critics agree we are no longer number one.

I feel the best way to document quality care is with outcomes. If a system can document excellent outcomes, why would you need to develop tracking criteria to be filled out with each visit? Just look at the organization's results regarding survival, hospitalizations, readmissions, and patient satisfaction. If the organization believes in God-given principles of honesty, integrity, hard work, striving for excellence, and developing a loving environment, I believe that outcomes will be superior and patient satisfaction will "knock your socks off" with approval. The early Christian communities demonstrated a paradigm from their time to love their neighbor. They learned that following that commandment changed the world and that following that rule made things happen. People became more likely to do the right thing for the right reason. I believe that a God-centered health care workers will do the right thing for the right reasons without regulations. The proof will be in the outcome of health care in this type of organization.

Currently, there is no such training in health care schools or postgraduate training programs to encourage developing these Godly principles. In our current culture, it is considered unethical to provide such training in regards to medical care. The "politically correct" dominate and propagate the exclusion of God and His precepts in the field of health care. I believe this is the cause of our downhill spiral in the field of medicine. We will continue on our downhill spiral until we get back to the basics of life: love your neighbor. Steve Jobs gave a great commencement address at Sanford University, "How to Live Before You Die," in June 2005. It spoke to me as I was writing this section. My wife was revisiting the speech on her iPad as I was writing this.

We can't look backward. We must look forward with optimism, faith, and trust in the idea that if healthcare workers follow the fruits of the Spirit, we will succeed. We just need a different forum and to follow a different road from the one medicine is taking. Return to the road from Troas where the evangelist Paul and the physician Luke joined forces and changed the world. I love my profession, as most health care workers do. All the current rules, regulations, and malpractice litigations have a tendency to pull us down. I feel these problems can all be improved if our profession allows for the development of the basic commandments of putting God in front and loving your neighbor as yourself. I love what I do. It is all the craziness of government regulations and constant threat of litigation that I dislike. If we develop a new concept where these principles are practiced, all these concerns will diminish.

I truly believe returning to God in the practice of medicine will make the difference. A book I recently read sums this up. It is in a great little book—*The Hermit* by David Torkington—and it applies to where I want to go. Torkington makes the following comment: "It is only when the dynamic rays of God's inexhaustible love begin to permeate the very marrow of our innermost being that we receive the strength to stand upright and grow, to ripen and bud under its influence, and finally to open out, to bloom forth. Without this source of light, we've no more chance of growing than a drooping geranium in a dark room." Yes, the answer to the very complex problems in the practice of medicine is very simple. It is love in all the elements of the practice of medicine. God is love, and we must involve Him in all parts of health care delivery to begin our recovery. Remember, Love and God is the answer. This concept will lead us out of the trap medicine has been ensnared.

Conclusion

Can you see how God has worked in my life? He has led me to do unusual and sometimes adventuresome things. Each time I prayed that my decision would glorify God, I hope it has. As I approach my seventy-fifth birthday, I have begun on a new adventure as a full-time cardiologist at the Veteran's Hospital. I have continued as chairman of the board of trustees of the new Seton Harker Heights hospital. I am also "called" to exert a large effort toward creating a new and hopefully better system of medical care, as well as to help build a new church in Salado. This new system I have called Troas Health Care will actually be a return to the old concept of medicine, when the patient–physician relationship was sacred and God was more apparent in that relationship. While maintaining excellence in science and in medical training, we need to focus on instilling in upcoming physicians a dominant role of compassionate care with a belief that God is ever present and a part of our medical decisions. This new system must focus on a "higher being" involved in the care of patients.

I realize under our current system it will require a huge miracle to accomplish the above described health care system. I have written this book to illustrate the many miracles that allowed a boy who wasn't supposed to get out of college to accomplish great success. I have done this all with God's help and a plan for His glory. I feel He will bless this concept of medicine so that physicians have an option to return to spiritually centered, compassionate care for all God's people. I hope my life demonstrates the glory of God. I feel that each miracle God gives to you requires that you use it in some way for His glory.

As stated in the beginning of this book, our current medical system has been led into a trap that has made us slaves to our health care reimbursement . All we need to do is have faith and trust in the Lord to be led out of the slavery that currently possesses us. We must separate from government and health insurance controls. I believe the Troas concept is the answer. This concept and my life recalls to mind the story of the ten lepers who were cured by Jesus (Luke17:11–19). I began this book with the question; I now end it with the question. Have you ever thought of what the one leper who was cured and returned to thank Jesus did with the remainder of his life? I have many times. I'll bet he did great things. It's too bad he didn't write a book. This book is a giant thanks to God for my life.

About the Author

Dr. Cashion has been a physician since July 1966. He attended medical school at the University of Texas Medical Branch in Galveston, Texas. He did internal medicine training on the Harvard Medical Service of Boston City Hospital. Cardiology training was completed at Georgetown University Hospital in Washington DC with the world-famous medical educator Proctor Harvey MD. Dr. Cashion later returned to the Harvard Service at Boston City Hospital and served as the chief medical resident.

Dr. Cashion served in the US Air Force on active duty at Scott Air Force Base during the Vietnam war. Following discharge, he practiced cardiology with Waco Cardiology Associates in Waco, Texas. He was then recruited to an academically affiliated group at Methodist Hospital in Houston, Texas. After nineteen years in Houston, he started a cardiology program in College Station, Texas. By the grace of God, he grew that program from a small community hospital to one doing interventional cardiology and open heart surgery. In 2005, he was recruited by Austin Heart to start an interventional cardiac program without surgical backup in Killeen, Texas. He was involved with the development of a community hospital in Harker Heights, Texas, seeing it develop from the initial idea into the fully functional Seton Medical Center Harker Heights—a community hospital with a four-star CMS rating. He currently serves as the chairman of the board of trustees of that hospital. He retired from Austin Heart to return to full-time cardiology at Olin E. Teague Veterans' Medical Center hospital in Temple, Texas. There he is involved with direct patient care and in teaching medical residents and cardiology fellows in training.

Printed in the United States
By Bookmasters